THORN, FIRE AND LILY

*Gardening with God
through Lent to Easter*

By the same author and published by Burns & Oates

GARDENING WITH GOD: Light in Darkness

THORN, FIRE AND LILY

Gardening with God
through Lent to Easter

JANE MOSSENDEW

BURNS & OATES
A Continuum imprint
LONDON • NEW YORK

Burns & Oates
A Continuum imprint
The Tower Building
11 York Road
London SE1 7NX

15 East 26th Street
New York
NY 10010

www.continuumbooks.com

Line drawings by Penelope Harter

First published 2004

British Library Cataloguing-in-Publication Data
A catalogue record for this book is available from the British Library

ISBN 0–8264–7064–5

Typeset by Bookens Ltd, Royston, Herts
Printed and bound in Great Britain by
MPG Books Ltd, Bodmin, Cornwall

*Dedicated to the Mother of Sorrows,
in memory of my grandmothers,
Ellen Banks and Sophie Mossendew*

CONTENTS

Part 1: LENT TO EASTER

Part 2: SOLEMNITIES AND SAINTS' DAYS

ACKNOWLEDGEMENTS

Copyright material is quoted by permission of the following: Stanbrook Abbey for 'Speedwell', Dame Scholastica Hegbin, O.S.B.; David and Charles for quotations from 'Folklore and Customs of Rural England', Margaret Baker (David and Charles, 1974); extensive reference to 'Flora Britannica', Richard Mabey, published by Chatto and Windus, used by permission of the Random House Group Ltd; quotation from 'The Donkey', G. K. Chesterton, by permission of A. P. Watt Ltd. on behalf of the Royal Literary Fund; quotations from 'The Culture of Flowers and Vegetables', Sutton and Sons, 1904, by permission of Suttons Consumer Products Ltd.; quotation from 'The House at Bethany', Rumer Godden, by kind permission of the Rumer Godden Literary Trust; quotation from 'Mending Wall', Robert Frost, used by permission of the Random House Group Ltd.; hymns quoted are from 'The New English Hymnal', used by kind permission of SCM-Canterbury Press Ltd.; Scripture quotations are from the Revised Standard Version of the Bible, copyright © 1946, 1952 and 1971 by the Division of Christian Education of the National Council of the Churches of Christ in the USA, used by permission. All rights reserved. Every effort has been made to contact copyright holders and any inadvertent omissions will be made good in future editions.

I should like to repeat my gratitude to those whose spiritual and/or temporal support is acknowledged in *Gardening with God: Light in Darkness*, and to add to them as follows: The Daughters of St Paul in Kensington, London; the Revd and Mrs John Farrant; Jackie and Alan Gear of the HDRA; Dave and Mon Holtom, Barwinnock Herbs; the Revd and Mrs Stuart Leamy.

Thanks also to Frances Garrett and Jonathan Childs for indispensable IT installation, help and advice; Jean-Michel Goumy, troubadour, for lightening life with his music; John and Sue Gregson, fence-builders against the depredations of marauding fowl; Maguy and Alain Jozeleau for their *amitiés* and many excellent meals from their *braisière* over the years; Val and Chris Ludlow for lasting friendship through thick and thin, and for all their help since Chris planted my thuyas in 1993, up to this year's building of water-feature, Way of the Cross and Empty Tomb of the Resurrection; my erstwhile news-vendor Steve of Sloane Square station, now happily market-gardening in Sussex, for friendly discussions about potato varieties; Monsieur Quanté, who holds mastery over weeds and grass during my absences from France; Margaret Wallis for her patient understanding and kind gift of red hollyhock seeds.

I have been privileged in warm appreciation and encouragement from Archbishop Cormac Murphy O'Connor of Westminster and Archbishop Rowan Williams of Canterbury. My heartfelt gratitude goes to both of them.

It has been a much-valued blessing that the five pillars of my creative, spiritual and personal life have remained unshakeable during the writing of this second volume in the 'Gardening with God' series, namely Martin Dillon, Penelope Harter, Paul Burns, Stephen Young and of course my husband, Colin Fulthorpe.

Saint Romain, 9 August 2003

Warning
Always consult a qualified medical practitioner before taking herbal remedies.

And plaiting a crown of thorns, they put it on his head.
(Matt. 27:29)

Therefore on this sacred night, receive, holy Father, the flame of this
evening sacrifice, which holy Church presents to you ... in the solemn
offering of this candle of wax, the work of bees. Now we know
the excellence of this pillar, which the glowing fire enkindles to the
glory of God.
(from the *Exultet* of the Easter Vigil)

My beloved has gone down to his garden, to the beds of spices,
to pasture his flock in the gardens, and to gather lilies.
(Song of Sol. 6:2)

INTRODUCTION

The first book of this series, *Gardening with God: Light in Darkness*,[1] closed on the eve of Lent, after a period of intense preparation for the season both in the garden and in church. This second volume follows a similar format, beginning on Ash Wednesday and concluding at dawn on Easter morning. A plant is chosen for each day and then related through its cultivation, history and lore to the major liturgical themes in Mass and Divine Office. As before, Part 2 is devoted to solemnities and saints' days that cannot be fitted in date sequence into the main liturgical cycle dealt with in Part 1. The idea is to use the two parts somewhat as one does the missal and breviary, turning on specific dates from the main seasonal liturgy to celebrate a Solemnity or to commemorate saints as their importance dictates.

Readers who are familiar with the first book will know that I describe a personal gardening and spiritual pilgrimage, and hope, through sharing insights that have been vouchsafed along the way, that others may reap spiritual benefit from their gardening experience. Those who will meet me for a second time in these pages will remember that, in 2001, on returning to my ruined French garden after an absence of almost three years I thought it would take at least five years to restore. Two years on, progress has exceeded all hopes and expectations. The ruination of exile gave the opportunity to rethink the overall design of the garden, and to deepen its spiritual symbolism. The long rectangular plot would henceforth be divided into six sections:

1. the Advent, Christmastide and pre-Lent enclosure;
2. a pleached 'Way of the Cross';
3. the 'Sanctuary' garden (the original herb garden);
4. the summer garden of Ordinary Time;
5. the autumn and winter beds of Ordinary Time;
6. nourishment and healing plot.

My dream is that eventually to walk round the whole will be to follow the cycle of the Church's year, both physically and spiritually. As I write, the first section is almost complete, except for the water-feature, planned for installation during the coming autumn, and 'The Way of Cross', to be put in place within weeks of finishing this book. The 'Sanctuary' garden has

xiii

taken on the aspect of a hidden woodland glade: the Calvary has been replaced, hundreds of bulbs put in, and wildflower seed sown about the pre-exile survivors. In its northeastern corner an 'empty tomb' of local stone is being built. And so the 'Sanctuary' is now, as one walks around it, first the 'Garden of Gethsemane', then 'Golgotha' and finally the 'Garden of Resurrection'.

In May, with the essential help of friends, we put up a rustic fence around the entire plot. The intention was to keep out the neighbours' marauding fowl, but it has had a profound effect on the atmosphere of the garden. Access to it can now be gained only through the French windows of my workshop, a large atelier that forms the southern boundary. Now, one goes into a totally enclosed little world, and the garden seems happier, safer, but able to speak its messages more clearly. Within its natural 'walls', I shall this summer, God willing, spend the long days working there and researching the third book of this series. It will be my annual six-week retreat from the world of curriculum frameworks, assessment objectives, grade criteria and all the rest of a teacher's lot, but I do not forget the outside world, nor you the praying gardener, for whom I pray, as in the Introduction to my first book, that you may find in your garden the healing peace and increased closeness to God that I find in my own.

J.M.
London, Feast of St Benedict, 11 July 2003

Part 1

Lent to Easter

LENT TO EASTER

ASH WEDNESDAY

CHAMOMILE *Chamaemelum nobile*; herb of humility; herb doctor; apple of the ground

Cultivation notes
C. nobile 'Treleague', a non-flowering variety discovered in Cornwall in the early twentieth century, is ideal for lawns and seats. A March Ash Wednesday is a good time to propagate by lifting, dividing and transplanting. New plants should be separated from clumps and planted out in their permanent positions or in pots of compost. The work is intricate and delicate, but the plants should reward you five-fold within the same number of months.

History and lore
The word 'chamomile' comes from the Greek *chamaimelon*, which means ground apple, and the plant must have been named from the scent released when the foliage is trodden underfoot. It is native to Europe and the Mediterranean regions and has been identified as one of the main constituents in the process of embalming Rameses II, who died in 1224 BC. Chamomile has long been set close to ailing plants as it seems to aid their recovery, and this is the reason it is called 'herb doctor'. It was one of the nine sacred plants of the Anglo-Saxons, and it has a long history as a strewing herb and as an ingredient in curative infusions for nervous tension and insomnia. In Tudor times chamomile was a favourite plant for making lawns and garden seats. In southern England today it can be found flourishing on cricket pitches and village greens, despite the necessary regular mowing and rolling.

Medieval illuminated prayer books often depict plants. Chamomile is beautifully represented in a border decoration in the *Hours of Anne of Brittany, Queen of France* (c. 1508). This exquisite volume, now in Paris at the *Bibliothèque nationale*, shows over 300 plants, with their names attached. It is a case of a Book of Hours becoming a Herbal. In the medieval past, plants were an added adornment in liturgical books; as a twenty-first-

3

century gardener, I use living plants to help me enter the daily liturgy and to explore its variety and depth of meaning.

Towards meditation

Whether Ash Wednesday falls in February or March, it is a good day to pay some attention to your chamomile. There is always meticulous weeding to be done and the activity helps us to focus on two of the major themes in the Mass and Office. The first of these is the threefold call to turn away from sin, to seek God's grace, and to grasp this day as the time for making a new start. One must find the weeds, identify the sins, and then weed the chamomile, weed the soul. The analogy continues if we reflect on the two natural methods of weeding. We can either dig the offender out by its root, or continually cut off its top growth, in the hope that lack of light will at last kill it. No gardener needs reminding of the tenacity of weeds, from the deep and thick-rooted 'in your face' vileness of dock to the insidious, crafty threat of mare's tail, both above and below ground. Similarly, no confessor needs reminding of the tenacity of sin. I think of mortal sin in connection with dock, and characterize the spread of mare's tail as the myriad little venial sins to which most of us are prone. The first cuts us off from God immediately and utterly; the second, if not dealt with, will have the same effect eventually. So, any time spent 'weeding' early in Lent should be beneficial to the chamomile and also to our self-knowledge and access to grace.

There is an old English saying: 'The chamomile shall teach the patience that rises best when trodden upon.' It must be this characteristic that led to its being named 'Herb of Humility'. The more you tread on it, the more it springs back; it does not whine, complain or argue. It just grows more healthily and strongly. And so chamomile brings us to another major theme in today's liturgy. Humility must be at the core of our Lenten fasting, almsgiving and prayer. Through the prophet Joel, God instructs: 'Rend your hearts and not your garments.' There must be no showing off, no drawing attention to our supposed sacrifices. St Clement in his letter to the Corinthians exhorts them to repent, but with humility of mind. And the humility itself must not be paraded. Chamomile is the perfect plant to remind us that the whole emphasis today is on inner sincerity, littleness and lack of show. And it culminates in the Mass Gospel reading from Matthew. Here, Jesus teaches that when we pray we must go into our room and lock the door. Attendance at Mass is a public act of prayer, but there is no point in it if we do not take that 'room' with us; receiving the ashes is a public acknowledgement of our mortality, but it is useless if we do not engage with that truth in our depths. We go from the church into the world with the sign of Christ's redemptive suffering on our foreheads. It is the one day in the year when the Church invites us to display publicly a physical mark of our allegiance to him, but our compliance is meaningless and profitless if the soul behind the dust-streaked brow is not in the 'private room' with God.

'Go into your room and shut the door and pray to your Father who is in secret; and your Father who sees in secret will reward you' (Matt. 6:6).

Bible readings
Isaiah 58:1–12: The fast pleasing to God; you shall be like a watered garden.
Joel 2:12–18: Rend your hearts and not your garments.
Psalm 51: Have mercy on me, O God ... Blot out my transgressions.
2 Corinthians 5:20–6:2: Be reconciled to God. Now is the time.
Ezekiel 18:30b–32: Repent; renounce sin; get yourselves a new heart and a new spirit.
Zechariah 1:3b–4b: Turn back from evil.
Daniel 4:2–4b: Make amends for wrongdoing; almsgiving.
Philippians 2:12b–15a: God is at work in you; no complaining or arguing.
Matthew 6: Jesus teaches us to pray.

Intercessions
For the sick and poor; for widows and orphans; for those in temporal and spiritual authority; for book illustrators; for gardeners and farmers; for agriculture in poor and underdeveloped areas.

For an increase in humility and the grace to make an honest, thorough examination of conscience, and to make a good Lent.

Place of spiritual retreat
In the 'private room' recommended by Christ, as in Matthew 6.

THURSDAY AFTER ASH WEDNESDAY

BORAGE *Borago officinalis,** herb of courage

Cultivation notes

Borage is an annual but self-seeds so readily that some people regard it as
a weed. However, if you need to start the plant off in your garden, now is a
good time to sow seed under cover, whether we are in February or March.
If you live in a warm southern area and borage has been present in your
garden before, you may have the delight of its blue flowers in spring
without further effort. It attracts bees and – of equal importance – deters
pests from strawberries and tomatoes, of which I grow a lot. The hairy
leaves are uncomfortable to handle, but pick the flowers as they open and
separate them from the calyx before use. Pull plants out after flowering if
you do not want them to pop up in inappropriate places next year.

History and lore

Borage is indigenous to the Mediterranean and possibly to the Middle
East. Some authorities think that it was probably introduced to southern
Spain by the Arabs, and others that it was brought to Britain by the
Romans. In any case it grows now in many parts of Europe, Asia and
North America, often in waste ground near human habitation. The Revd
C. A. Johns, in his *Flowers of the Field*,[2] explains 'borage' as a corruption of
the Latin *corago* (*cor* = heart, and *ago* = bring, agitate or rouse). When
one remembers its use as a stimulant in drinks, perhaps his explanation is
not so far-fetched. Another more common suggestion is that it comes from
Latin *burra*, meaning a hairy garment, because of its leaf texture. But in
spite of these possible derivations, I like to think that the English borage
and the French *bourrache* both come from the old Celtic *borrach*, meaning
courage. If this is true, borage could have been brought to Gaul and
thence to Britain in early Christian, perhaps even pre-Christian, times.
Whatever the truth, it has long been known as the 'herb of courage', and
ladies would embroider its bright blue flowers on the jerkins of knights
about to depart for the Crusades. And, indeed, there is an old English
saying: 'I Borage bring alwaeis courage.' Pliny called it *euphrosinum*
because of its euphoric effect, and it has been traditionally used against
depression. Gerard, in *The Herball* (1597), tells us to 'use the floures in

* *Officinalis* in a plant's name means 'having uses'.

sallads to exhilarate and make the minde glad. There be also many things made of them, used for the comfort of the heart, to drive away sorrow, and increase the joy of the minde.' The flowers, usually available from May to September, certainly have a cooling effect on liquids, and their mild cucumber flavour and aroma enhance Pimms and other summer drinks. The leaves are rich in mineral salts and can be used in cooking if you wish to reduce salt intake.

Towards meditation

Later in the year, the vibrant blue of borage will turn my heart and soul to Our Lady, but today its five petals call to mind the five wounds of Christ and its leaves the 'hair-shirt' of Lent. The association of the plant with courage will lead me to consider how I go about 'putting on' that shirt. Weakness and self-indulgence dictate a need for courage in persevering with the miserable little sacrifices I have decided to make. How is the necessary courage to be acquired? Not surprisingly, because it is almost totally compiled from the Word of God, today's liturgy answers the question perfectly. At the first Office of the day we read about the oppression of Israel in Egypt. During this, the midwives are put to the test when they are ordered by the Pharaoh to kill all baby boys born to Hebrew women. Fear of the Lord gave them courage to disobey. If we acknowledge God's power, he will give us the strength to refuse to do things that we know to be wrong.

Fasting is a problem when your job is physically, mentally and emotionally demanding; almsgiving is a problem when you have little or nothing to give and are struggling to pay the bills. Pope St Leo the Great in today's second Office reading sets us right: for fasting, he says, eliminate bad habits; for almsgiving, concentrate on works of mercy. We may not be equal in financial resources but we can be equal in the love we feel and demonstrate to others, even if it is only in small acts of kindness and tolerance. His advice is sound, as long as it is not used as an excuse to deny ourselves nothing at all, or as a cover for meanness.

At Mass, the readings continue to show the way to courage. Moses sets the choice before the people of Israel and before us. It is the choice between life and death, blessing and curse. If we choose life we shall, as the Psalmist says, meditate on God's law night and day and be happy because we trust in the Lord. This is the trust that inspires our courage. In the Gospel, Christ speaks directly to us: if you trust me, he says, and wish to follow me, you must take up your cross daily. It is that 'daily' that strikes me. He knows that most of us would be well advised not to promise more than a day at a time. So every morning in Lent I say to myself and to God: today I will try not to complain; today I will try not to snap back with the clever put-down; today I will try to spend time with someone whom everyone else ignores or avoids. In the face of the suffering world, and of his agony above all, this is pathetically little, but it has to be better than doing nothing.

At Prayer during the Day, Paul enjoins us not to throw away the confidence we have been given because we need the endurance it will give us to do God's will and benefit from his promises. I am reminded of C. S. Lewis's comment that courage is always present when any other virtue is being tested. At Evening Prayer the letter of James tells us to resist the devil and he will flee from us.

December 2002 was very rainy and mild in southwest France. Even so I was amazed on the eve of 2003 to find several borage plants beginning to flower near the broad beans. When I left a week later there still had not been a frost, but I dreaded it for them. 'They will be gone when I return', I thought. Nevertheless, the sight of those brave and tender petals in the depth of winter taught me the lessons of courage yet again. My prediction about the frost proved correct: according to my neighbour, a $-12°C$ freeze in February had done away with the borage and also the normally hardy broad beans. The latter were a sad and irreplaceable culinary loss that year, but during the week before Palm Sunday I found a solitary borage growing in the drive. It was beginning to flower, and, knowing the risk, I could not resist transplanting it to the Lent garden. A fortnight later it was erect and happy in its new position. Yet again the saying 'I Borage bring alwaeis courage' proved true as I prepared to climb the mountain of coursework-marking and form-filling on my return to London!

So for courage, there we have it. Fear of the Lord; control bad habits; love more and do not be mean; choose life; read the scriptures; be happy in the faith and the trust God gives; take up the cross daily; hang on to your confidence in God; resist evil; and – I humbly add – be open to the message borage sends as a reminder of all this. 'We are not of those who shrink back, but of those who have faith and keep their souls' (Heb. 10:39).

Bible readings
Exodus 1:1–22: The oppression of Israel in Egypt.
Deuteronomy 30:15–20: I set before you a blessing and a curse.

Joshua 1:9: Let not your heart be troubled.
Psalm 1: Meditate on his law day and night.
Psalm 39: Happy the man who trusts in the Lord.
Hebrews 10:35–9: Do not throw away your confidence.
James 4:7–8: Resist the devil and he will flee from you.
Luke 9:22–5: Deny yourself; take up the cross daily.

Intercessions

For those whose courage is being severely tested by torture and persecution; for midwives; for those suffering from depression and mental illness, and for all who care for them; for close attention to the liturgy so that we may gain from it the riches God has placed within it; for discernment as to the right direction of our individual Lenten offering.

Thanksgiving for the lives and work of the patriarchs, prophets, evangelists, apostles and Fathers; and in modern times for the life and writings of C. S. Lewis.

Place of spiritual retreat

Facing Christ, as in Luke 9: What is my cross today?

FRIDAY AFTER ASH WEDNESDAY

BULRUSH *Cyperus papyrus*; *Scirpus*
'BULRUSH' *Typha latifolia*; great reedmace

Cultivation notes

The second plant listed above is the
one commonly thought of as the bulrush,
but it has in fact usurped the name.
The misconception came about because
the Victorian artist Lawrence Alma-Tadema
painted it instead of *Scirpus* in his *Moses
in the Bulrushes*. The work was famous, and
with the passage of time his mistake
became accepted as fact. The female flower
head of *Typha latifolia* is the familiar dark

brown cylinder borne on tall stems and contains thousands of minute flowers. The great reedmace is deciduous and perennial. It grows to a height of seven feet and is not suitable in a small domestic setting. In a large garden pond try *T. laxmanii (T. stenophylla)*. This has grey-green foliage and produces small 'pokers' between June and October, reaching a height of three feet. For a small pond, *T. minima* seems the only option. This grows to a height of 12–18 inches, has rush-like foliage and produces flowerheads that are the shape of large, elongated acorns.

For the purist, *Scirpus* is the true bulrush, and happily it is suitable for domestic ponds. *S. lacustris* grows up to four feet in height, has needle-like leaves, and produces small brown flowers toward summer's end. For a smaller variety try *S. Zebrinus*, whose two-to-three foot stalks have green and white horizontal spangles. Divide clumps of both *Typha* and *Scirpus* in spring.

History and lore

The invasiveness of the bulrush is borne out by the belief that parts of the Nile were completely covered by it at the time of the Pharaohs. And apparently just before World War II it was a menace in the marshland at the north end of the Plain of Gennesaret. The Egyptians are said to have made paintbrushes from its smaller stalks by carefully fraying one end, and poor Ethiopian children chew the slightly liquorice-flavoured roots even today. The bulrush has a formidable rooting system that prevents it from being washed away by moving water. It is known that the roots were strong enough to make handles for baskets that would need to bear quite heavy weights. In England its seeds were once used by poorer country folk to stuff mattresses.

If you do not have a pond you can buy *T. latifolia* already dried; if you grow your own, collect in midsummer. Look for young specimens to avoid the seed heads bursting. These can be recognized by their lighter brown and by the fact that they still have part of the infloresence on their tips, like a candle wick. Cut off the spikes and air dry as soon as possible, then store for use in dried arrangements.

Towards meditation

The story of Moses and the bulrushes is told again today in the Divine Office. 'And when she could hide him no longer she took for him a basket made of bulrushes, and daubed it with bitumen and pitch; and she put the child in it and placed it among the reeds at the river's brink' (Exod. 2:3).

Reading this story every year leads me to reflect on the several ways in which Our Lord was hidden during his life on earth. First, he is sheltered in the security of Mary's womb; after the Flight into Egypt, he hides there with his mother and Joseph until danger is past; his childhood is almost completely hidden from us; during his public ministry there are several occasions when he slips through crowds, effectively hiding himself, because his time has not yet come; his identity is hidden from Mary Magdalene on Easter morning until he speaks her name; and it is also hidden from his disciples on the road to Emmaus, until later, when, after he has expounded the scriptures to them, they recognize him in the breaking of bread. We too continue to recognize him, hidden though he is in the altar tabernacle under the form of bread. At every Holy Communion he calls each one of us by name; we too know him then and say to him, '*Rabboni*' (Master). Reflection on the possible reasons for all these different concealments will bear fruit, but at this stage in my thoughts I have several times experienced a tremendous upsurge of joy; when gardening on these occasions I have burst spontaneously into song with '*Adoro te devote*', 'O Bread of Heaven beneath this veil', or 'Sweet Sacrament Divine'. Thomas Aquinas's magnificent plainchant *Pange lingua* is saved for Maundy Thursday.

But today it is Friday, and indoors this evening there will be time to make a Lenten wall nosegay or vase arrangement. Small bulrushes will be employed among the bay, eucalyptus and rosemary, and handling them will remind me of their use in making writing material at the time of the prophets. My King James Bible upbringing comes to the fore here and I automatically think of Isaiah's reference to 'the paper reeds that grow by the brook' (Isa. 19:7). My mind then moves to Ezekiel's literal and spiritual consumption of the scroll, prefiguring the ways in which we may partake of the Word (Ezek. 3:3ff.). This morning I was filled with wonder and gratitude to God for the Blessed Sacrament. Now, guided by the day's liturgy, I dwell awhile on the need to read and listen to God's Word. Here again there is cause for profound awe and thankfulness. Some years ago I was in my herbary saying Morning Prayer when I was overcome with such love for the Word, which the Office contains, that I almost stopped breathing. The volume lay in my hands, apparently an inanimate artefact, and yet it seemed to me that it lived and breathed in a way no other book does, except of course for the Bible itself. The Word lay in my hands and I realized it that day. Ever since then I have embraced the Office as another kind of Holy Communion. Of course, being human, I do

11

not always pray it with proper attention. But that love is still there, still deeply felt, still a wonder, still a grace; and however tired or distracted I am, as long as I approach it with all the concentration I can muster, something of value is given. It may be a new insight; it may be a chastisement; it may be a stiffening of the backbone; it may simply be a blessed balm to my weariness. It may be many other things . . . but all are signs that God is nourishing me through the Word.

Returning to the bulrush and the specific demands of Lent, I remember Isaiah's image of a man formally bowing his head but not understanding the nature of fasting that is acceptable to God (Isa. 58:1–9): 'Is such the fast that I choose, a day for a man to humble himself? Is it to bow down his head like a rush and to spread sackcloth and ashes under him?' In this, today's first reading at Mass, God goes on to answer his own questions in no uncertain terms, and the rest of the liturgy interprets and consolidates his message: one's fasting is only acceptable if it is accompanied by works of mercy and concern for the poor. At Prayer during the Day, James exhorts us to confess our sins to one another and to pray for one another: 'The prayer of the righteous man has great power in its effects' (James 5:16b).

In yesterday's Office of Readings Leo the Great guided our thinking about fasting and works of mercy: it is not a question of the magnitude of the action but of sincerity and generosity of spirit in the doing. Today John Chrysostom examines the prayer that is a matter not of words but of a constant state as we go about our work. This type of prayer is a gift of the Holy Spirit, and John describes it as 'heavenly food'. He advises us how to prepare our souls to receive it. Think, he says, of your soul as a house, which you decorate with modesty, humility, justice, good works, faith and generosity. Then place prayer overall as the roof of the house so that the complete building will be ready to receive the Lord.

So I set out on the Lenten journey invigorated and helped by the liturgy to attempt the right relationship between prayer, fasting, good works and the partaking of the Word through sacrament and scripture. It is a question of balance, I think, standing back to appraise my work on the Lenten nosegay, and as my eye lingers on the bulrushes they offer a final message in the Latin tag, *in scirpo nodum quaerere* (looking for knots on a bulrush stalk). So, not too much navel-contemplation. Look always toward God and toward his poor. 'Of course I am unworthy', I think, tidying up the workbench. 'All the more reason', comes the answer, 'to get on with the pursuit of "religion that is pure and undefiled before God and the Father ... To visit orphans and widows in their affliction, and to keep oneself unstained from the world"' (James 1:27).

Bible readings
Exodus 2:1–12: The birth and flight of Moses.
Isaiah 55:3: Incline your ear, and come to me; hear, that your soul may live.
Isaiah 19:9 (AV): The paper reeds by the brook.
Isaiah 58:1–9: Is it to bow down his head like a rush ... ?
James 1:27: Religion that is pure and undefiled.
James 5:16: Confess your sins to one another.
Matthew 9:11–13: When the bridegroom is taken away, then they will fast.

Intercessions
For musicians, artists, and the makers of musical instruments and artists' materials; for those in the paper and printing industries; for better stewardship of trees and natural resources.

For all in flight or in hiding from persecution; for a curbing of our desire to know things that are not our business; that the Lord may help and guide us in our Lenten observance and that he may open our eyes, ears and hearts to receive him; for deepening sincerity in prayer and action; for those who seem deaf and blind to God.

Place of spiritual retreat
With the disciples of John the Baptist, when they ask Jesus why his disciples do not fast, as in Matthew 9.

SATURDAY AFTER ASH WEDNESDAY

BURNING BUSH *Dictamnus fraxinella*; dittany (white dittany)

Cultivation notes
The modern bush is the summer-flowering *Dictamnus albus*, which has orange-scented foliage. It is hardy, but it does not take kindly to transplantation, so, if you are not fortunate enough to have one already, it may be better to sow the ripe, hard, black seed in groups in late summer and be patient. Dittany likes well-drained alkaline soil in sun. Mulch

13

annually in late spring and cut back to ground level in autumn. It will grow to a height of about two feet and produce its white, blue, red or striped flowers on long spikes in summer.

History and lore

Dictamnus is possibly named after *Origanum dictamnus* (dittany of Crete), which in turn is probably named after Mount Dikte in Crete. It is first mentioned in Chinese medical sources in about AD 600. Today it is found on dry scrubland and among pine trees from eastern Asia to southwest Europe. It is rich in oils, which are exuded in vapour from glands that cover the plant. In hot, dry and cloudy conditions this vapour can spontaneously ignite, leaving the bush undamaged. Be careful of it in hot summer weather. Bark peeled from roots lifted in autumn can be used to make an external wash for scabies, eczema and arthritic or rheumatic pain. *Note: Avoid in pregnancy.*

Towards meditation

The place on which you are standing is holy ground.
(Exodus 3:5)

If you have an established bush, visit it today and cut out any frost damage, being careful to avoid living wood. Even if you do not have a *Dictamnus* you may like to ponder its connection with the burning bush of Exodus. The Hebrew word *seneh* translates literally as 'thorny bush'. In the New Testament, when the story of Moses and the bush is referred to, the Greek word used is *batos*, which appears to mean bramble (Mark 12:26; Luke 20:37; Acts 7:30, 35). The word *seneh* is reputed to have given the meaning to the Wilderness of Sin, as well as to Mount Sinai. Obviously the self-combustion of dittany, which leaves it unharmed, has led to its association with the biblical subject. The idea has been dismissed by those of a practical mind because dittany does not burn long enough to be the bush of scripture. Yet others have suggested that it may have been the crimson-flowered mistletoe which, when the sun shines through its host, may look like fire. It is hard to accept that Moses would have mistaken the parasite plant for a real burning bush. Surely the main points here are that God could have used any bush he wished, dittany or not, for the purpose of appearing to Moses and calling him; and we can use the modern shrub to remind us of the spiritual meaning of the incident. Significance not science is the byword here. In Exodus 3:2 the angel of God precedes him, as the Hebrew translates, 'in the mode of a flame'. I take the flame to convey the unapproachable holiness of God, and that it declares the living holy God as the Indweller. It is the background of God's promise of his presence to Moses, of the keeping of the covenant with the fathers, of the divine name and of the holy law of Sinai. Several avenues of thought open up here: for instance God's calling of sinners (cf. yesterday's readings) and therefore of us, and our response; or meditation may turn to contemplation even though we, like Moses, are afraid to look.

Bible readings
Exodus 3:1–20: The call of Moses; the revelation of the holy name of God.
Isaiah 44:21–2: Come back to me for I have redeemed you.
Isaiah 58:9–14: Your light will rise in the darkness.
Revelation 3:19–20: If one of you hears me calling.
Mark 9:1–14: The Transfiguration of Jesus.
Luke 5:27–32: I have not come to call the virtuous.

Intercessions
For sufferers from skin disease, arthritis and rheumatism.

For members of contemplative religious orders; for biblical scholars; for help in discerning God's way for us and for strength to follow it; for a quiet waiting for God; for mercy and forgiveness for ourselves from God, and to others from us; thanksgiving for God's revelation of himself, and for his love for us.

Place of spiritual retreat
With the disciples after they had been told by Christ not to speak of what they had seen at his Transfiguration as in Mark 9.

15

FIRST WEEK IN LENT

FIRST SUNDAY IN LENT

LAMB'S EAR *Stachys byzantina* (*S. lanata*; *S. olympica*), lamb's tongue

Cultivation notes
This mat-forming perennial is probably so popular because of its evergreen foliage, which looks good in a silver border. The small, pink tubular flowers appear in summer and are borne on woolly upright spikes. Lamb's ear grows to a height of from 12 to 15 inches in a well-drained sunny position. An excellent groundcover plant, it can be sown or planted in spring. *S. lanata* is good for large areas, but there are other varieties, including *S. macrantha* (*S. grandiflora*) and *S. nivea*, which both have purplish-pink flowers. There is also the smaller *S. lavandulaefolia*. This can be quite rampant and needs space to spread. It produces beautiful silky purple-red flowers. All enjoy full sun.

History and lore
Stachys is native to rocky hillsides from the Caucasus to Iran and was introduced to Britain in 1782. Its common names clearly came about because of its woolly-textured, spoon-shaped leaves.

Towards meditation
I know my own and my own know me.
(John 10:14)

Lamb's ear cannot fail to remind me of Christ the Good Shepherd, and of us who, in the words of the Book of Common Prayer General Confession, 'have erred and strayed from thy ways like lost sheep'. But he has rescued us in the most profound way, by laying down his life for us. Thoughts will also stay awhile with those of no faith and with the sheep 'not of this fold'. The liturgy today emphasizes our need for bodily and spiritual food and water, telling the story of Jesus being looked after by the angels during his fast and temptation in the wilderness. We are fed by God's bounty in nature, but also by his word, by the sacrament of Communion and by his love and care for us.

16

Then there is the symbol of Christ himself as the Lamb of God. At some point today, even if I do not listen to them on CD, I am bound to hear in my head the strains of the Glasgow Orpheus Choir singing 'All in an April Evening', a favourite on the radio request programmes of my youth. 'I saw the sheep with their lambs and I thought of the Lamb of God.' Every time we go to Mass we appeal to him under that name to have mercy and to grant us peace. Significantly, we do this just before Communion, and then the priest holds up the Host and tells us, 'This is the Lamb of God who takes away the sins of the world. Happy are those who are called to his supper.' As I plant lamb's ear along the Lenten border of my garden 'Way of the Cross', my mind will be ranging over these mysteries, and I will select one to concentrate on when I have finished my physical work for the day.

Lamb's ear, then – a low-growing but useful plant both practically and spiritually. It is strange but often the case that lowly plants often produce more fruit in prayer than other majestic, beautiful and fragrant ones. But then we should not be surprised since Jesus himself told us, 'The last shall be first and the first shall be last.' So even as we leave it, this commonly seen groundcover plant holds out a final important reminder.

Bible readings
Genesis 9:8–15: God's covenant with Noah.
Isaiah 53:8: He was led as a lamb to the slaughter.
Isaiah 40:11: He will feed his flock like a shepherd.
Psalm 23: The Lord is my Shepherd.
1 Peter 3:18–22: That water is a type of the baptism which saves you now.
Matthew 4:4: Man does not live by bread alone.
Mark 1:12–15: Jesus was tempted.
Matthew 18:10–14: The Lost Sheep.
John 10:1–18: The Good Shepherd.
John 1:29: Behold the Lamb of God.

Intercessions
For shepherds and all who work in sheep-farming or wool industries.
    For the hungry, thirsty and homeless; for those who have lost their way.
    That we may work for the common good; that we may hunger and thirst for spiritual food and drink.
    For an increase in self-control; for deeper attention to preparation for Holy Communion.

Place of spiritual retreat

In the wilderness with Jesus, as in Mark 1.

MONDAY WEEK ONE IN LENT

ALEXANDERS *Smyrnium olusatrum*
(*Petroselinum alexandrinum* in medieval
Latin); black lovage; black
pot herb; horse parsley

Cultivation notes

This hardy biennial
(occasionally perennial)
grows to a height of four feet.
It is a lover of coastal regions,
and inland favours chalky soil. It is not to be confused with angelica or
lovage, from which it can be distinguished by its glossy, bright green
leaves, which are not deeply indented. Its flowers, which appear between
April and July, are bright lime-green, whereas those of lovage are white or
pinkish. Propagate Alexanders by seed or planting outdoors in early
spring. A sunny site and rich, moist, sandy soil are preferred.

History and lore

Alexanders is a native of Macedonia, the country of Alexander the Great,
and the plant's name perhaps derives from the fact that, when pulled
back, the leaf-shield has the shape of a helmet. *Smyrnium* is from the Greek
word for myrrh, and the plant could have been so named because of the
aroma and flavour of some of the species. *Olus* is Latin for vegetable and
atrum is black – an obvious reference to the seeds. The medieval Latin
name means Alexandrian parsley, so it would seem the plant originated in
the Mediterranean region. It was known to Theophrastus in 322 BC, and
Pliny described its cultivation as a pot herb in the first century AD. It is
thought to have been brought to Britain by the Romans, and its leaves,
roots, top stems and flower-buds all feature in medieval recipes. The
young flower-buds, for instance, were pickled like miniature cauliflowers.
Sailors took dried leaves on long voyages as a protection against scurvy. It
was cultivated as a vegetable in medieval monastic gardens, and colonies
can still be found growing wild by the ruins of old abbeys and castles in

Ireland and England, notably at Steepholm in the Bristol Channel, site of a twelfth-century Augustinian monastery; and at Elstow in Bedfordshire, not far from an abbey of Benedictine nuns founded around 1078. Colonies are also present above cliffs near Dover, as well as in Norfolk and on the Isle of Wight.

In the seventeenth century Alexanders was known as Macedonian parsley, and the seed was sold under that name by apothecaries. Culpeper,[3] who classifies it as a herb of Jupiter, and therefore friendly to nature, claims also that 'it warmeth a cold stomach and openeth a stoppage to the liver and spleen'. Anise and fennel seem to have overtaken it in popularity as a digestive, and it is generally not now in medicinal or, indeed, culinary use. Coles (1656) recommends that the roots stewed or eaten raw with vinegar would 'in time of Lent help to digest the crudities and viscous humours that are gathered in the stomach by the much use of fish at this time'. So if it is your Lenten habit or rule to abstain from flesh meat for protracted periods you may like to grow Alexanders to use in the making of a soothing soup, to mix the flower-buds in salads and grind the root as a digestive condiment. The leaves are a pleasant addition to a white sauce, and the flower-buds make an unusual salad ingredient. The stems are celery-like in texture and can be cooked like asparagus, which of course is much more fiddly to grow and expensive to buy.

Harvest from established plants – leaves, stems, and buds in spring and early summer, roots in autumn, seeds when almost black. Store seed for culinary use, or keep for sowing in spring. Autumn sowings tend to give larger stems the following year.

Towards meditation

> Though I fail, I weep:
> Though I halt in pace,
> Yet I creep
> To the throne of grace.
>   (From George Herbert, 'Discipline')

If the weather is sufficiently spring-like, make a sowing today or put in a bought plant. This year I planted two which began life in Ayrshire and seem all the better for that in a French garden. The 'auld alliance' is not dead it seems. As I planted them my mind conjured the deserted monastic ruins where their English and Irish relations still grow in profusion, places where for centuries our ancestors in religion applied to their souls the hard practice of the strict Lenten fast. In our own time the visionaries at Medujorge claim that Our Lady has exhorted the faithful to fast three days a week, throughout the year, for their individual spiritual benefit and in reparation for sin. When I first read of this, I was daunted, until I considered that if to fast is to take one meal in the evening with wine allowed and a snack during the day, then I fast every day of the year in any case. But each year I must ask how much self-denial am I applying? Surely it must involve more discomfort than I experience in my normal regime to count as true fasting? And so I try to measure what I do against its effect. Is it enabling me to 'turn with greater freedom to the thought of God and virtue'?[4] Is it proving to be, as spiritual writers call it, one of the wings of prayer? Is it increasing my love and concern for others? And if it is, am I showing it in a practical, immediate way, regardless of how much is in my Lent box? (There is today the same emphasis in the liturgy as there was yesterday on this aspect of fasting.)

For many years now I have found that my pre-Lenten plans become overlaid by what seem to be God's demand for sacrifices and endurances of a different and unforeseen nature, and that the whole season does in fact provide at least the beginnings of affirmative answers to my questions. So now, each new Lent I start out with my own tentative plan, an open mind and a strange mixture of confidence and dread.

Bible readings
Isaiah 58:1–11: The fast that is pleasing to God.
Matthew 4:1–11: Jesus fasts and is tempted in the wilderness.
Matthew 6:16–18: Outward behaviour when fasting.
Luke 18:9–14: The Pharisee and the tax collector.
Mark 12:41–4: The widow's mite.
Matthew 25:31–46: As you did it unto the least of these ... you did it unto me.

Intercessions
Thanksgiving for the resources of the earth; for those who govern, that they may preside over a fair distribution of those resources.

Forgiveness for past self-indulgence; strength and grace to persevere in our Lenten observance; for self-control and a curb on wastefulness, extravagance and materialism; for generosity according to our means.

For the grace to bring joy and comfort to those in need; for unblinkered eyes and unblocked ears to recognize what God is asking of us this Lent.

Place of spiritual retreat
In the Temple with the archetypal Pharisee and tax collector, as in Luke
18.

TUESDAY WEEK ONE IN LENT

ALMOND *Prunus dulcis*

Cultivation notes
The almond will flourish in any reasonable garden soil and likes the sun.
It can grow to a height of 30 feet and produces its pink blossom in March
or April before its leaves. Depending on the forwardness of the season,
today may provide an opportunity to plant.

History and lore
In Asia Minor reverence for the almond predated the birth of Christ by
at least a millennium. The Greeks regarded it as a symbol of fruitfulness
and believed that Phyllis, wife of the Athenian king Demophon, turned
into an almond tree after committing suicide because she thought he had
abandoned her. The almond, now the world's most widely grown nut
tree, was cultivated for its fruit in western Asia and Mediterranean
regions in ancient times. It has been grown in Britain since the sixteenth
century, and the wood has been traditional in the making of tool handles
and in ornamental carving. (It is possible that St Joseph knew the
qualities of its hard, pale-red timber.) Almond oil has long been valued
in perfumery and is a soothing agent for sunburn. Nutritionally ten
almonds are equal to half a pound of meat. (Always blanch or roast the
nuts before eating, and remember that they can be poisonous if
consumed in large quantities.) British summers are not normally warm
enough for the nuts to ripen fully, and the tree is more often grown for its
blossom, which is the cheering harbinger of spring, sometimes appearing
as early as February. Appropriately the Hebrew word used in Jeremiah
and Numbers is *shaqed,* meaning 'waker' or 'hastener', and in the
nineteenth-century *Language of Flowers*[5] it signifies hope. There used to be
some growing in the school playground opposite our church, but they
were uprooted in the 1990s to make way for a housing development for
the rich. No longer is the gloom of late winter lifted by seeing them from
the bedroom window. Fortunately I had a photograph of them in full

21

bloom; this is now in the church archive as a permanent reminder of the parish's loss.

Towards meditation

My word shall succeed in what it was sent to do.
(Isa. 55:10)

Traditionally, the almond represents promise; ecclesiastically it signifies divine approval or favour, and sometimes the Blessed Virgin. The reasons are not hard to find in Jeremiah (1:1–12), where God promises to watch over his word and perform it, and in Numbers (17:8), where Aaron's rod of almond flowers and fruits, thus making public his status as God's chosen priest and also that of his descendants within the tribe of Levi. (The rod was so honoured that it was kept with manna and the tablets of the Covenant: Heb. 9.)

The almond, then, is a tree blessed of God, and among the many thoughts it provokes is that only God can give life, even where it seems impossible. This can lead to an interpretation of the almond blossom as the Virgin Mary, and the fruit as Christ. Another thought is that only God can choose who will lead and be a blessing to others. This may lead to a reflection on the priestly calling. In John's Gospel the imagery used by Jesus when talking of the calling of his disciples mirrors that which surrounds the call of Aaron: 'You did not choose me, but I chose you and appointed you that you should go and bear fruit and that your fruit should abide.'

So the almond has led us to think of Jesus, our true hope and our true High Priest, the embodiment of God's fulfilment of his promises in the old covenant, and the unfolding of his plan of salvation. This will lead us to recall the promises of Christ himself: that we shall not be left desolate; that he will come again and take us to himself; that the Counsellor, the Spirit of truth will come to us and keep the Word alive in our minds; that if we love him, the Father and he will love us and dwell with us; that if we ask, our sorrow shall be turned to the fullness of joy. The long address by Jesus after the Last Supper as recorded in John is greatly comforting, but Jesus makes frequent use of the word 'if'. In Lent I pay special attention to those conditionals. Nevertheless, we should have no hope at all were it not for Christ, and so when I plant my almond in France later in the year that will probably be the uppermost thought in my mind. And when I see it in blossom for the first time, Swinburne's 'winter's rains and ruins are over' will take on a joyful spiritual significance.

Bible readings
Isaiah 55:10–12: My word shall succeed.
John 14:1–31: Jesus' address after the Last Supper.

Intercessions
For those who work in the cultivation of the almond tree and its products; for carpenters and toolmakers, and all who use wood in their craft or art.

Thanksgiving for plants that supply perfume and oil for healing ointments.

For those who have lost hope; for a strengthening of our own hope; for priests and for vocations to priesthood and lay ministry; for an increase in love both in prayer and action.

Thanksgiving for God's love and for our salvation.

Place of spiritual retreat
Listening to Jesus speak, as in John 14.

WEDNESDAY WEEK ONE IN LENT

HORSE-RADISH *Armoracia rusticana*; red cole; raifort

Cultivation notes
The invasiveness of this perennial is well known, both above and below ground. I once heard the suggestion that it should be grown in a bottomless bucket placed on an impenetrable slab of stone or concrete. The tap-root is cut for culinary use as it emerges. Strangely, horse-radish has belied its reputation in my French garden and failed to establish itself strongly, and I have therefore not needed to employ such restrictive practice. In Sutton's *The Culture of Vegetables and Flowers*[6] we are advised to dig up the whole crop annually, store it in sand and then use a new planting spot in each successive year. It seems to me that unless you are superhumanly thorough, this approach would positively encourage rather than deter propagation.

Since the plague of the potato grubs in 1995[7] I had not attempted to grow potatoes. This year, however, I have put in a few rows of second earlies in the hope of having them during the long summer holiday, and because of the reputation horse-radish has of being a good companion in the potato patch, I am trying again to get it to flourish there. Perhaps, as is often the case with companion plants, their proximity will be mutually beneficial to tuber *and* root.

History and lore

Amoracia is the Latin name for the related wild radish, and its root verb means to equip, arm, kindle or inflame. Horse-radish, native to west Asia, contains vitamin C and gave relief to sufferers from scurvy and to sailors deprived of fresh vegetables. It is listed in the Mishna (a rabbinic law code) as one of the bitter herbs of Exodus 12:8. It is thought to have been introduced to Western Europe by invading barbarians in the fifth century, and the Slavs supposedly began to cultivate it as early as the twelfth century. Its date of arrival in Britain is unknown, but it was certainly here by 1548 when William Turner remarked that 'It groweth in Morpeth ... And there is called redco.' Fifty years later Gerard recommends it as being preferable to mustard as a condiment, and in fact it contains mustard oil. He tells us that the Germans used to eat it with fish, and the French sometimes refer to it as '*moutarde des allemands*'. Horseradish is strongly diuretic, but is also an appetite stimulant and aids digestion. There is an old recipe for the relief of rheumatism, which recommends swallowing (without chewing) tiny unbruised pieces of the root over a period of four weeks. Horse-radish tea has been recommended as a spray for apple trees at the first sign of attack by brown rot.

Aficionados of gardening according to lunar phases claim that the roots are keenest when dug by the light of a full moon! However that may be, the root's savage assault on the tearducts when it is being grated can be counteracted by freezing beforehand, or by holding a thick piece of good dry bread between the teeth. (Strong onion fumes can be similarly absorbed.) Alternatively, if your sinuses need clearing, forget the bread. The nineteenth-century chef Alexis Soyer invented an awesome horse-radish sauce recipe: 'Universal Devil's Mixture'. Apart from the horse-radish, the ingredients include chilli vinegar, cayenne and black pepper, and chopped chillies. He suggests it be pressed into incisions made in the meat, which is then slowly broiled, and for the last few minutes as near as possible to the 'pandemonium fire'! Perhaps a little much for all but the most intrepid. My own recipe is simpler and consists merely of fresh, grated horse-radish, mustard powder and single cream. It is nevertheless very hot, and those unused to it have to be warned.

Towards meditation

> Let my tongue cleave to the roof of my mouth, if I do not
> remember you, if I do not set Jerusalem above my highest joy!
> (Psalm 137:6)

Horse-radish is an example of a plant reminding me of a person, and you may like to choose as today's subject another 'bitter herb' that has connotations of exile. However, horse-radish always reminds me of my paternal grandmother, and of her garden where nothing else grew. Born on a Cambridgeshire farm in the mid-nineteenth century, she was the first woman to qualify as a teacher in that county. Her career ended with marriage, for in those days women were not allowed to embrace both vocation and sacrament. My grandfather was an employee of the London and North-eastern Railway, and after the birth of four children the family was posted from Peterborough to Sheffield. There my grandmother remained for the rest of her long life, in an exile of uncomplaining sacrifice, a quarter of a century of which was a patient, dignified widowhood. Not for nothing did we sing John Keble's 'Blest are the pure in heart' at her funeral.

That horse-radish came to hold sway in her garden was a family joke, the point of which was probably the irony of a countrywoman in the city unable to rear anything in the ungenerous city soil. Certainly, my grandmother never laughed at it, and I never once saw her gardening. I have since suspected that she could not bear to face the comparison between the productive loam of Fenland and her small, rank patch in Sheffield. 'How can we sing the Lord's song in a strange land?' Outwardly she appeared dour and passionless, but I saw the gleam in her eye when she read letters aloud to me from her sister in Wisbech – letters about how the hens were laying, how the pigs were farrowing, and, as the year turned, about the volume of strawberry, apple and plum harvests. When samphire had been gathered we knew of it as soon as the post could convey the news. Oh how I wish I had those letters now!

Have I strayed a long way from prayer here? I think not: if the receptive ear of a child gave my grandmother comfort, I offer thanksgiving for that, and for everything she taught me to value and recognize, not the least how to make Yorkshire Pudding and to know the difference between a damson and a bullace, and between a Bramley seedling and a Grenadier. Every time I think of her, which is often, it is in a spirit of sympathy, gratitude, love and admiration. Perhaps she dreamed of going home permanently one day, in which case the horse-radish, being one of the 'bitter herbs' of Exodus, was highly appropriate. I will end today by listening to Palestrina's setting of '*Super flumina Babylonis*'.

'Lord, let all exiles know your care for them: may they find their homeland once more, and come one day in joy to the Father's house.'[8]

Bible readings
Exodus 10: In the plague of darkness the children of Israel had light.
Exodus 12: The Lord's Passover.
Psalm 137:1–6: If I do not set Jerusalem above my highest joy.
John 21:16–19: Where thou wouldst not go.

Intercessions
For farmers; for fruit- and potato-growers, especially those in Cambridge-shire; for married women teachers; for railway workers.

For patience, fortitude, endurance; for mutual tolerance and kindness between young and old; for exiles and refugees; for the souls of our beloved dead.

For our faith, that like the horse-radish root it may strike deep and spread wide.

Thanksgiving for the lives and influence of our relatives.

Place of spiritual retreat
With the risen Jesus and his disciples, as in John 21.

THURSDAY WEEK ONE IN LENT

AGRIMONY *Agrimonia eupatoria*; church steeples; guardian of the fields; sticklebur; cocklebur; fairy's wand or rod; Aaron's rod

Cultivation notes
Throughout the summer this common wild perennial bears its small star-shaped, slightly apricot-scented flowers on tapering spikes that grow to over two feet in height. These are attractive to bees and butterflies and often do not open until the bristly, nodding fruits begin to appear on the same spike. The fruits have a ring of hooks that catch on animal fur and human clothing to ensure seed dispersal. The plant is a graceful and ecologically helpful addition to the summer border, where it will enjoy

well-drained soil and full sun and will be tolerant of dry conditions. Its root-system dredges up valuable nutrients from deep in the soil. Sow seed in late summer or plant in autumn.

History and lore

Agrimonia is from the Greek *argemon*, meaning a white mark on the cornea, a condition the plant was reputed to cure, and for centuries this herb has been used to treat eye complaints. Another derivation is from the Latin *agri moenia*, 'defender of the fields'. *Eupatoria* refers to King Mithradates Eupator of ancient Persia (first century BC) who is thought to have discovered the virtues of agrimony and introduced its medicinal use. He is supposed to have taken a small daily amount of poison in his search for an all-purpose herbal antidote. The Anglo-Saxons regarded agrimony as a heal-all, but it was particularly important as a wound herb. Later, the medievals put it under their pillows for a good night's sleep. In the fifteenth century it was an ingredient in *Eau de arquebusade*, a preparation used to treat wounds inflicted by the musket (arquebus). William Coles, Nicholas Culpeper, Sir John Hill and Doctor Losch between them accredit it with the power to ease a tremendously long list of ailments and wounds, including snake and rabid dog bites (Coles); pulling out splinters and strengthening dislocated joints (Culpeper); jaundice (Hill); and tonsilitis and angina (Losch). Culpeper also remarked that if people knew its sight-restoring qualities, opticians would go out of business. In North America John Josselyn (seventeenth century) mentions it as growing wild in New England, and it was used by native Americans for treating fevers.

Agrimony contains vitamins and tannin, but is not regarded as a culinary herb. Nevertheless, in Western and oriental folk medicine it has for centuries been an ingredient in most herbal teas. In the past the plant was used to make expensive tea go further, and in the present day agrimony tea is recommended to treat kidney and bladder ailments, gastroenteritis, gall and liver malfunctions and sore throats. It is an aid to digestion and helps to control diarrhoea, so it should be avoided by those with a tendency to be constipated.

As a rule, the whole of the plant is used except the root. Harvest before the fruits form and tie in bunches of five or six stems. Hang them upside-down in the airing cupboard or other warm, dry place. When the flowers and leaves are dry and crisp put them through a parsley mill and store in screw-top jars away from the light. Aside from tea, a gargle can be made with two large handfuls of stems, leaves and flowers to a quart of boiling water. Applied externally a double-strength infusion relieves sprained muscles. For the home-dyeing enthusiast agrimony is the source of a pretty yellow dye for wool. In the past, its tannin content led to its use in the dressing of leather.

Towards meditation
The liturgy today concentrates on the dual identity of Christians as members of Christ's flock and, in our attempt to follow his example, as shepherds of others. Agrimony, under its common name 'church steeples', keeps the first aspect in mind. In the Old Testament Office reading we revisit the first Passover celebration and recognize ourselves as descendants of the children of Israel; at Morning Prayer a passage from 1 Kings again reminds us 'we are your people, Lord, and your heritage'; at Evening Prayer James tells us to be 'God's true subjects', to stand firm against evil and to come closer to God, who will then come close to us. We should be 'steeples' constantly pointing ourselves towards him, and in so doing bear him witness in the eyes of the world. The Mass emphasizes another aspect of our relationship with God in the Church. We should rely on God as our true helper (Esther 4:17) and should give him praise and thanks for the times he has strengthened us and come to our rescue (Ps. 137). In the gospel, Christ himself tells us that if we ask, we shall receive.

Considering agrimony as 'guardian of the fields' leads me to reflect on today's second Office reading in which St Asterius (died c. 400) concentrates on our role as shepherds of other people. King Mithradates made me think of faith, hope and love as the antidote to the poison of unbelief, despair and hatred. But like Paul most famously before him, Asterius singles out love as of prime greatness. He exhorts us to 'meditate carefully on the richness of Christ's charity' because it is only through trying to emulate it that we can even approach the state of being truly loving. If we study how Christ received sinners we will learn to be non-judgemental; if we try to imitate him as shepherd we will learn to be considerate, kind and untiring in our care for others. We will realize that no one is lost or beyond hope, and therefore constantly stretch out our hands to those who wish to return to our community, or to those who wish to join it for the first time. We have been forgiven, so must we forgive. 'Let us be shepherds after the style of Our Lord' (St Asterius, Homily 13).

Bible reading
Exodus 12:1–20: The Passover celebration.
1 Kings 8:51–53a: They are thy people and thy heritage.
Esther 4:17: I have no helper but you.
Psalm 137: On the day I called you answered.
James 4:7–8: God's true subjects.
Matthew 7:7–12: Everyone who asks receives.

Intercessions
For more love and forgiveness in our communities and personal relationships; for greater loyalty to God and more reliance on him.

Thanksgiving for the healing properties of agrimony and of all medicinal plants.

Place of spiritual retreat
With the disciples as Christ taught them, as in Matthew 7.

FRIDAY WEEK ONE IN LENT

HYSSOP *Hyssopus officinalis*

Cultivation notes
This perennial shrub is evergreen in mild winters and grows to between eighteen inches and four feet in height. Its rich blue flowers produced in August are borne in the leaf-axils on one side of the stems. It likes sun and well-drained alkaline soil and appreciates shelter. Plant two feet apart in spring (or twelve inches apart for a hedge). In mild-winter areas cut back to eight inches after flowering, otherwise do this in spring. Replant after two or three years if it becomes straggly. Bees and butterflies are very fond of it, so plant where it will lure the Cabbage White away from your brassicas and radishes. It is reputedly a good companion plant for the grapevine and can also be grown indoors.

History and lore

The Greek *hyssopos*, used by Hippocrates, may derive from the Hebrew *azob* (holy herb). It was used for purifying temples and ritual cleansing of lepers. According to Jewish law, persons, things or places that had been defiled had to be cleansed by purifying water; the sprinkler was often a bunch of hyssop dipped in the purification water. The argument over the true identity of biblical hyssop is still not resolved. Many authorities maintain that it was a form of oregano, savory or thorny caper. However, common hyssop is again in favour in some quarters, particularly since the discovery that the mould which produces penicillin sometimes grows on the leaves. The ancient Greeks boiled it with rue and honey to make a cough mixture, and Pliny (first century AD) mentions a wine known as *hyssopites*. St Augustine thought of it as a short-stemmed rock plant whose roots could penetrate deeply between boulders and the stones of walls. Tenth-century monks brought the herb into central Europe, where they used it to flavour liqueurs. To this day it is an ingredient in Chartreuse and Benedictine, and it has been a favourite in monastery gardens for centuries. It appears in Alexander Neckam's list of 1199 and so was a possible newcomer to Britain at that time.

Thomas Tusser and William Coles both recommend it as a strewing herb, the latter listing 15 varieties in his seventeenth-century herbal, whilst John Ray in his *First British Flora* (1670) records the story of a man kicked by a horse, who applied hyssop. Not only did his pain disappear within hours, but there was no trace of bruising afterwards. The nineteenth-century Dr Losch suggests its use in 'fumigations to relieve humming and buzzing in the ears'. In the Victorian *Language of Flowers* hyssop signifies cleanliness, another case of the compilers following a biblical lead, although perhaps misguidedly in this case, as we have seen. Hyssop is naturalized in North America as far south as North Carolina and as far north as Quebec. American country folk are said to use it to soothe painful bruises and contusions and in external treatment of muscular pain.

In modern British herbalism hyssop tea is given for rheumatism, and green tops in soup are given to help asthmatics. In small amounts the leaves aid digestion and increase appetite. Flowering tops are infused to treat lung complaints, bronchitis and catarrh. The oil is applied to bruises, and is valued in perfumery and aromatherapy. Hyssop gives a wonderful flavour to honey, and dried leaves add a pleasant fragrance to sachets, hop pillows and pot pourri.

Harvest on a sunny day and place in cardboard trays for two to three days until dry; store in screw-top jars.
Note: Do not give to epileptics, and avoid in pregnancy.

Towards meditation

Hyssop is an obvious choice for a day when the liturgy concentrates on purification and repentance, and it matters neither jot nor tittle to me that our common hyssop may not be the plant mentioned in Exodus 12:22 or Psalm 51:7. I am conditioned to visualize common hyssop when I read these texts. What matters is that hyssop leads me to reflect on two things.

The first is the importance of water in church ritual, particularly its use during the sprinkling of the congregation before High Mass, with its accompanying plainchant setting of the Psalmist's, 'Purge me with hyssop and I shall be clean ...' Every time I am present at this rite, I feel a sense of connectedness with the Old Testament, for Mosaic prescriptions constantly refer to the use of water. A large metal basin of clean water, known as the 'sea of brass' stood in the court of the Temple. Priests and people washed themselves in it before crossing the threshold, and even before their private prayers. After the example of Jesus' baptism in the Jordan, the Church continued to make use of the symbolism of water at a greater spiritual depth. Whereas in the Old Covenant water ritualistically washed away breaches in the law, the holy water of the New Covenant washes away the stain of sin.

There are several kinds of holy water in Catholic liturgy, but 'the water of aspersion' or ordinary holy water is what interests me today. This is the water used in the stoups at the entrance to our churches, and at the asperges, or the *Vidi aquam* of Eastertide. It is tempting to imagine that the practice of sprinkling the faithful has an unbroken history from Moses to the present day, and that the aspergillum, in fact a perforated ball at the end of a handle, is still a bunch of hyssop. There is a tradition that St Matthew recommended the use of holy water to attract converts from Judaism by using a rite with which they were already familiar. Why should we suppose that he and they were insufficiently aware to appreciate the deepening of divine metaphor? The first detailed account of the use of holy water seems to be in the Pontifical of Serapion (fourth century), the blessing of the water described therein bearing great resemblance to the formula still used today. However, the earliest reference I can find to the asperges is in the letters of Hincmar of Rheims (806–82), in which he records a synodal dictate: 'Every Sunday before

High Mass each priest should proceed to bless water in a clean vessel worthy of its lofty purpose; he should sprinkle the people . . . ' According to the *Liber Usualis*, the plainchant tune normally sung at the asperges dates from the thirteenth century, whilst that for the *Vidi aquam* dates from the tenth.

The Church uses salt in holy water because it was a Jewish custom and because of its symbolism. As water is used to quench fire, so salt is used to preserve from decay. They are combined in 'the water of aspersion' to express the reasons why it is used. The two-fold purpose of ordinary holy water is to purify and protect, and this is clearly expressed in the ancient prayers that sanctify it. I find them beautiful; those said over the salt invoke the power of 'the living God, the true God, the holy God', so that evil may depart from any place where it is sprinkled, and that whoever is touched by it shall be sanctified and freed from all uncleanness and attacks from the powers of darkness. The prayers said over the water are addressed to the Blessed Trinity and ask that evil may be utterly expelled from the world and lose its influence over us. Then God's blessing is asked for the water, that wherever it is sprinkled there may be freedom from disease and the snares of Satan. As the priest puts the salt into the water in the form of the cross, he prays: 'May this mingling of salt and water be made in the name of the Father and of the Son and of the Holy Ghost.' God is then asked to sanctify the salt and water, so that wherever it is sprinkled the Holy Spirit shall be present.

The sprinkling of water is all about praying for protection from evil, for resistance to temptation to sin; but my second consideration today is of the Gospel and second Office readings. These lead to a reflection on the specific condition that we must fulfil before we can even express our sorrow for sin already committed. It is no use coming to God if we have an unresolved argument with someone or have affronted someone and not apologized or asked for forgiveness. St Aelred, in the second Office reading, reminds us how petty most of our differences are when held up in the light of Christ's example. On the cross he prayed for his enemies, 'Father forgive them.' That is remarkable enough in itself, but he also made the excuse for them, that they were ignorant. They do not know the identity of the One they have crucified, 'for they know not what they do'.

And so I leave the hyssop, taking away a renewed and more lively appreciation of the asperges and the *Vidi aquam* and a resolution to forgive and make excuses for others rather than myself. As poems to read in this context, I recommend George Herbert's 'Repentance', 'The Sinner' and

'Unkindnesse', Gerard Manley Hopkins's 'Bad I am and yet thy child', and for music the plainchant setting of the *De profundis*.

Bible readings
Exodus 12:21–36: The Plague on the first-born of the Egyptians, 'Take a bunch of hyssop and dip it in blood ... '
Ezekiel 18:21–8: When the sinner renounces sin he deserves to live.
Ezekiel 47:1–9: Water was issuing from the right side of the Temple.
Psalm 129: Out of the depths I cry unto thee.
Matthew 5:20–5: Go and be reconciled with your brother first.

Intercessions
For beekeepers, viticulturists, and monks who make liqueurs; for those who work in the perfume and aromatherapy industries; for sufferers from rheumatism, muscular pain, bronchitis, asthma, catarrh, eating disorders, poor digestion; for lepers.

For true sorrow for sin every time we are sprinkled with holy water, or see the hyssop plant; that we may pray more constantly for the banishment of evil from the world; for tolerance and forgiveness of others; for grace to make the first move in settling differences.

Place of spiritual retreat
With the disciples listening to Jesus' teaching, as in Matthew 5.

SATURDAY WEEK ONE IN LENT

NIGELLA DAMASCENA love-in-a-mist;
love-in-a-puzzle; Jack-in-prison;
devil-in-the-bush
NIGELLA SATIVA nutmeg flower;
black cumin; Roman coriander

Cultivation notes
Love-in-a-mist is the most commonly
grown *Nigella* in domestic gardens. It is
an elegant hardy annual that is easily
propagated. Sow in flowering position in
spring or autumn (although it seems to benefit

from early sowing). Thin to nine inches apart. It likes a sunny, open site, where it usually grows to about 18 inches. The English name must have been inspired by the fine upper leaves that encircle the flowers. These appear in summer and are often blue, with 'Miss Jekyll' and 'Miss Jekyll Dark Blue' probably the most popular. 'Persian Rose' is a creeping variety. The seeds are aromatic and apparently slightly narcotic, so it is important to distinguish it from *N. sativa*, which is widely and safely used as a spice. Also an annual, this has white, blue-tinged flowers and grows to about 12 inches in height. The fruits have wavy green horn-like styles. It appreciates similar conditions to those required by *N. damascena*.

History and lore

N. damascena arrived in Britain from Mediterranean regions around 1570. *Nigella* is the diminutive of the Latin *niger*, meaning black, an obvious reference to the seeds; *damascena* was originally thought to derive from Damascus. Gerard gives it the Anglo-Saxon name *gith*. It produces an essential oil used in the manufacture of lipstick and scent.

    N. sativa is referred to in the Old Testament as 'fitched' from the Hebrew *ketzah* (vetch). For centuries it has been a popular spice in India, Turkey, Greece, the Middle East, and especially in Egypt and Tunisia. Before the introduction of pepper it was important as a condiment. It came to Britain about the same time as *N. damascena*, and was first grown at Syon House on the banks of the Thames in west London. In France, the seeds were crushed with cinnamon, coffee or chocolate and used to flavour cream. In England the seeds were burned to ashes and mixed with pork grease. This paste was then combed through hair in the belief that it would get rid of lice. Nowadays it is most commonly used to flavour a wide range of foodstuffs, from bread to cooked vegetables. The oil is extracted as a substitute for spikenard. Medicinally, it has a laxative effect and is prescribed to ease period pain and to increase milk in nursing mothers. Harvest the seed when ripe and dry for later extraction of oil, or to use in infusions ground or whole.

Towards meditation

Three aspects of the *Nigellas* explain their choice today. The first is the rather revolting image conjured by the pork fat and charred black cumin seed. But it also reminds me of Isaiah's symbolism at Morning Prayer: 'Wash, make yourselves clean, take your wrongdoing out of my sight.' The second is the connection that the oil of *N. damascena* has with make-up, and therefore with mask, disguise, illusion, self-delusion and vanity, and with our determination to alter ourselves to fit in with whatever is the current worldly notion of beauty. I have nothing against make-up as such: heaven knows I have worn enough of it myself on stage over the years, whilst pretending to be someone else. But I sometimes worry for my girl pupils, who now as early as nine years of age seem expert in its application as a fashion accessory. By the time they are 15 they spend every available minute in front of the mirror outside my classroom, behind the stage of our theatre school. Ineffectually, I joke with my girls that they will wear out the mirror. 'What's *inside?*' I ask them. What indeed? Fear of being 'uncool' in many cases, and vacuity in others. Whose fault is it? Society at large, peer pressure, multinationals, fashion gurus, loss of religion? All of these I think. It is certainly not the fault of the girls themselves. They are to be pitied more than criticized. They are only following the example of adults totally absorbed with the 'body and face beautiful'.

Older women who cannot accept the decline of their physical beauty also come to mind: my father's older sister was firmly in that category, and he would often quote to me, in affectionate compassion about her:

> Poor flesh, to fight the calendar so long;
> Poor vanity, so quaint and yet so brave;
> Poor folly, so deceived and yet so strong,
> So far from Ninon and so near the grave.[9]

Sympathy and concern for women like this, and of course for my girls, leads me to think of their plight as symptomatic of the third reason I have chosen love-in-a-mist. We live today in a veritable fog of concentration on physicality; but the second reading at the Office today, from the documents of the Second Vatican Council, examines our condition and what should be our proper aspiration. The extract reminds us that only Christ can show us the way to be worthy of our destiny. He is the key, the purpose and the true love and beauty at the centre of all. In our mad world of flux and 'progress' he is the same yesterday, today and forever. Faith in him enables us to see through the mist, to the most important reality, symbolized for me by the flower of today's plant, and that is that the more closely we follow Christ, the more genuinely we try to imitate him, the more truly beautiful we will become. This is the only beauty that really matters in the end, and so my final contemplation of the *Nigella* prompts me to an assault on any sham or vanity in my life. God alone sees how beautiful or ugly I am.

Bible readings
Deuteronomy 26:16–19: You will be a people consecrated to the Lord.
Psalm 118: They are happy who follow God's law.
Isaiah 1:16–18: Wash, make yourselves clean.
Isaiah 44:21–2: I have dispersed your faults like a cloud.
Galatians 6:7b–8: If he sows in the field of self-indulgence.
Revelation 3:19–20: Look, I am standing at the door knocking.
Matthew 5:43–8: Be perfect just as your heavenly Father is perfect.

Intercessions
For the soul of Gertrude Jekyll, and those of all the dead who made gardens during their lives on earth.

For nursing mothers; for sufferers from gynaecological problems; for inner cleanliness; for the vain and vacuous that they may be opened to things of the spirit; for our young people; for a more constant awareness of reality in Christ; for awareness of our own faults; for a spirit of humility; that we may increasingly reflect the beauty of Christ.

Place of spiritual retreat
Reflecting with the disciples, as in Matthew 5:48.

SECOND WEEK IN LENT

SECOND SUNDAY IN LENT

MULLEIN *Verbascum thapsus*; hag taper; high taper; torches (torch blade); Our Lady's taper; Aaron's rod; Jacob's staff; Peter's staff; candlewick; bird's candles

Cultivation notes
This ancient and usually biennial plant runs up to four or five feet when preparing to put forth the single, and beautiful, yellow flower-spike in the summer of its second year. The leaves at the base can be a foot long and very shaggy, reducing in size towards the top of the plant. Soft, fine hairs on leaves and stems protect it from moisture loss, insects and grazing animals. Raindrops from smaller leaves fall on the lower ones and so on down to the roots. Mullein will self-seed, but otherwise sow seed in autumn or spring, or take root-cuttings. Beware of caterpillars!

History and lore
Mullein is found throughout Europe, except in the northernmost parts, southwest Iberia and the Alps. The Latin name was given by Pliny, and the English is thought to derive from the French *molène*. Indeed, if you translate most of the English folk names literally into French, you will be understood (e.g., *Cierge de Notre Dame*). The ancients believed it to have magical properties, and it was given to Ulysses to protect him from Circe, who changed his crew into pigs. The Romans called it *candelaria*, and their soldiers are believed to have used mullein stems dipped in grease as torches on the march. 'High taper' comes from its similar use at high festivals of the Medieval Church. 'Hag taper' is possibly from the apparent popularity of the plant among witches. The Anglo-Saxon for hedge is *hoeg*, and one wonders whether the name was given because witches were supposed to shelter under hedges or whether witches were hags because of that habit. Whatever the truth, 'taper' is an appropriate name for the tall spike of mullein with the golden yellow fire of its flower.

Abbot Aelfric mentions it in his list of 200 plants of Britain (AD 995), and before the arrival of cotton it is believed to have been picked by penitents who scraped the downy substance from the leaves to make candle-wicks. And the soft thickness of the leaves led to their being used as footwear insoles. The soft texture probably earned the name 'Adam's Blanket'. According to Katherine Oldmeadow, in *The Folklore of Herbs*,[10] Sir Walter Scott always rewarded a person who told him a new word. Oldmeadow did likewise and recompensed with a shilling the gypsy who referred to mullein as 'blanket leaf'.

Culpeper recommends powdered mullein leaf tea for coughs and croup, and powdered flowers as an analgesic and sedative. Macerate them in olive oil in a sunny place for three weeks, and strain before using to control inflammation in the ear. (Administer two or three drops, twice or three times a day.) The preparation has also been traditionally used to treat bruises, frostbite and haemorrhoids. The crushed dried leaves have a pleasant fruity smell and were once smoked to control a hacking cough. Most parts are poisonous if taken internally, but dried flowers have been used to make cough medicine. In the United States also, the downy leaves are an old folk remedy for chest complaints, and the oil is used for ear problems. Dian Buchman in *Herbal Medicine* (London: Herb Society and Random Century, 1981) recommends five drops of the flower oil in a teaspoon of cold water to control bedwetting in children.

Always gather in dry weather and avoid crushing the petals.

Towards meditation

The key words in the history and lore of mullein that link it to the themes of today's liturgy are: *march*; *torch*; *fire*; *penitence*; *light*; and *glory*. Since the day after Ash Wednesday we have been following in the first Office readings the history of the Israelites, from the call of Moses through to the oppression in Egypt, the Passover, and then the departure from that land. Today we go with them as far as the Red Sea, and the mullein reminds me of how God led them constantly on their march, in a pillar of cloud by day and a pillar of fire at night.

Turning to the Mass, we read first of Abraham's near-sacrifice of Isaac and are reminded that the event foreshadows God's sacrifice of his Son to atone for the sins of the world and for the sins of each one of us, profound sorrow for which is rightly at the heart of all our Lenten practice. Then in the psalm and second reading, the Church responds to the Exodus text of the Office, promising to 'walk in the Lord' and offering thanksgiving to him because he has freed us from bondage; and in Paul's words gives voice to her confidence in God. But it is with the gospel that the symbolism of mullein is even more strikingly appropriate, for it is Mark's account of the Transfiguration.

In the second Office reading St Leo offers two reasons why Christ chose to show his glory to the disciples: first, the memory of it would bolster their faith in the face of the imminent disgrace of the Cross, and second that the presence of the patriarchs would tie the incident to the old covenant and fulfil it. The Old and New Testaments are both lights that guide us. At the Transfiguration they fuse into a single glorious flame.

Bible readings

Exodus 13:17–14:9: The Lord went before them ... in a pillar of fire to give them light.
Psalm [116]: I will walk in the presence of the Lord.
Romans 8:31–4: With God on our side who can be against us?
1 Thessalonians 4:1–7: Against sin.
Mark 9:2–10: The Transfiguration.

Intercessions

For sufferers from the complaints that mullein has traditionally been used to treat.

For greater gratitude for God's constancy; for more frequent prayer to the Holy Spirit; for a deeper sorrow for sin; for a heightened awareness that our faith too is bolstered by the Transfiguration, and of the fulfilling nature of the New Testament in relation to the Old.

Place of spiritual retreat

With the disciples after the Lord's Transfiguration, as in Mark 9.

MONDAY WEEK TWO IN LENT

WORMWOOD *Artemesia absinthium*

Cultivation notes

This hardy deciduous shrub grows to a height of between two and four feet and has beautiful silky foliage. It likes full sun and bears yellow flowers in August. Take semi-hardwood cuttings in late summer and prune in autumn. Wormwood is a good fungicide if planted between currant bushes and fruit trees, and near henhouses it can deter lice. Do not plant near fennel, sage, caraway or other culinary, medicinal herbs. Rainwater washes a toxin from the leaves that seems to inhibit growth of other herbs. It does, however, repel flea-beetle and Cabbage White butterflies. 'Lambrook Silver' is a good choice if growing for the beauty of leaves.

History and lore

According to legend wormwood sprang up in the tracks of the serpent as it crawled out of Eden; aside from rue, it is the bitterest of herbs. Biblical references are to *A. judaica* or *A. herba alba*. It is mentioned seven times in the Old Testament, where the word is the Hebrew *laanah*, and twice in the New Testament, with the Greek word *apsinthos*. The reference in Revelation could indicate that the word meant 'undrinkable'. All species have a strong, bitter taste, leading to the symbolism of sorrow or calamity (Prov. 5:4; Lam. 3:15, 19; Amos 6:7, 12). Moses used it to show the perils of secret idolatry (Deut. 29:18), and Jeremiah as a warning of the punishment awaiting disobedient Israel (Jer. 9:15; 23:15). After the death of the Persian/Greek king Mausolus in 353 BC, his wife Artemisia built a tomb for him and this became one of the seven wonders of the world. (It is from this that our word 'mausoleum' is derived.) Artemisia was also a botanist and medicinal researcher, and I cannot help but think of her when looking at plants of the *Artemesia* genus. In the ancient Greek text of Dioscorides, wormwood is mentioned as a cure for internal worms, and the ancients used it variously as a hangover cure, a diuretic, a tonic digestive, an appetite restorer, an antidote against vegetable poisons and a guard against seasickness. In Anglo-Saxon lore it was one of the nine sacred herbs for fending off evil. In 1557 the British herbalist Thomas Tusser praised its several uses:

> While Wormwood hath seed get a handful or twaine,
> To save against March, to make the flea refraine.
> Where chamber is sweeped and Wormwood is strowne,
> No flea for his life, dare abide to be knowne.
> What saver is better, if physick be true,
> For places infected than Wormwood and Rue.
> It is as a comfort, for hart and the braine,
> And therfore to have it, it is not in vaine.

Indians from New Mexico to British Columbia use it to treat bronchitis and colds, whilst in Chinese tradition a leaf is rolled and inserted in the nostril to stop nosebleeds. In the *Language of Flowers* it is listed as symbolizing absence, possibly from a misunderstanding of word derivation.

In Wales, it was used instead of hops to flavour beer, and it is an ingredient in various vermouths. The word 'vermouth' comes from the German *Wermuth* (Anglo-Saxon *wermod*) which originally meant 'preserver of the mind'. However, as many nineteenth-century addicts of absinthe found to their cost, it is in fact quite the reverse, unless one interprets 'preserver' as 'pickler'! Absinthe was first made by Henri Pernod in 1797, and its consumption became a serious problem in Europe and North America, to the extent that in 1908 it was banned from various countries after its addictive properties had been identified and it had become apparent that excessive use led to hallucinations and damage to the central nervous system. Dégas (1834–1917) painted *The Absinthe Drinker*, showing a young girl at a café table tasting the bitterness of absinthe. It is a permanent reminder of the danger of the drink and is eloquent of sadness, pensiveness and regret.

Apply strong wormwood tea to bruises and with rue and sage, in pulped form, to spider, scorpion and jellyfish bites and to wasp and bee stings. Add a sprig to any leftover white wine and then steep for a fortnight; it can then be used as an insecticide, reputedly most effective against moths and other flying insects. A powder can be made from ground leaves. Hang sprays in grain stores to deter beetles and lay branches between onion and carrot rows against carrot and onion fly; infuse for a strong household disinfectant. The silvery leaves are stunning in moonlight and enhance bouquets, wreaths, wall nosegays or tussie-mussies. Boil stems to produce a yellow dye. Pick the flowering tops and leaves in mid- to late summer and then dry.

Note: Avoid internal use during pregnancy.

Towards meditation

The history and lore of wormwood are full of symbolism that matches the themes and realities of today's liturgy. In the first place it is associated with sin through the legend of the serpent crawling from Eden, but in the first Office reading God parts the waters of the Red Sea for the Children of Israel to cross over, in obedience, to safety from the Egyptians. Moses, their leader, foreshadows Christ and the way in which, through the cross, he parts the sea of sin and opens the gates of heaven to us. According to Matthew, before crucifixion Christ was offered an anodyne of gall and vinegar, and gall has come into our language together with wormwood as a metaphor for any bitter or painful experience. It is thought that the mixture he was offered was a diluted wine containing stupefying drugs, so it is possible that wormwood was very close to the cross. Both Matthew and Mark tell us that Jesus refused the libation. He elected instead to drink to the last dregs the chalice of human pain and sin, the chalice of obedience to his Father's will, without the assistance of any painkiller or mind-numbing drug. As well as appalling physical pain he chose to endure an indescribable mental and spiritual anguish. And through that very endurance we are able to drink the chalice of salvation. I reflect that obedience like this is given only to the martyrs. The rest of us must look on in humble awareness of how much less God wants from us in our ordinary lives. He wants us to repent, to listen to him, to avoid excess and the temptation of what is bad for us; to seek pardon for sin, to reorientate our attitudes, to care for others and, in imitation of his mercy towards us, to have mercy likewise on them.

In the second Office reading St John Chrysostom helps me to clarify my thoughts today. It is an extract from his *Instructions to Catechumens*, among whom I count all Christians. From it I take two thoughts for continued reflection: (1) the Jews cast off a foreign yoke; I must cast off the galling slavery of sin; (2) the Lord walks at my side because of my obedience.

Bible readings
Exodus 14:10–31: The crossing of the Red Sea.
Exodus 19:4–6: Obey my voice, keep my covenant.
Psalm 102:10: Do not treat us according to our sins, O Lord.
Isaiah 58: Care for others.
Ezekiel 18:23: God wants us to renounce sin and live.
Romans 12:1–2: Let your minds be remade, your nature transformed.
Hebrews 11:25–7: Moses refused sin with his eyes on God's reward.
Luke 6:36–8: Be merciful, even as your Father is merciful.

Intercessions
For the health of our plants; for botanists and medicinal researchers; for addicts and substance-abusers and the work of Alcoholics Anonymous; for all who suffer physically, mentally and spiritually; for greater care and love for them; for greater mercy and tolerance.

For reorientation of our attitudes, and an ability to recognize and give up our 'secret idolatries'; for strength to resist temptations and self-indulgent, damaging excess.

Place of spiritual retreat
In the crowd listening to Jesus teaching, as in Luke 6.

TUESDAY WEEK TWO IN LENT

Manna ash *Fraxinus ornus*

Cultivation notes
A fully-grown manna ash has a more rounded shape than common ash (*F. excelsior*) and has denser foliage. The leaves can be up to a foot long, and the tree can grow to a height of 30 feet, though often much less. The bark is smooth and grey, and the flower-buds are pale brown. The scented creamy-white flowers are borne on large, showy heads and appear from April to June. Bunches of winged fruits follow until as late as September, when they will begin to turn brown. Like most ashes the manna is fast growing and tolerates a wide range of conditions.

History and lore
The manna that God fed to the Children of Israel during their journey through the wilderness was once thought to be the gum produced by manna ash. This is edible and sweet and seeps from cuts in the trunk. It dries into whitish flakes on contact with the air. However, ashes are native to central Europe and the Mediterranean and do not grow in desert regions. Tamarisk is now believed to have been the possible source of the divinely given food of Exodus.

In Italy and Sicily the gum of manna ash has been collected since the fifteenth century, and in 1929 an Italian law reserved the name 'manna' for the product made from it. It is thought to have been introduced to Britain around 1700, and John Keats (1795–1821) is probably referring to it in 'La Belle Dame sans Merci': 'She found me roots of relish sweet, / And honey wild and manna-dew ... ' In modern Britain it is often planted in parks and gardens for its early summer flowering.

Start tapping the gum only when the tree is eight years old. In a warm, dry summer make a series of slanting incisions on alternate sides of the trunk. Scrape off the 'manna' when it has solidified. Commercially this gum is an ingredient in mild laxatives for children and for pregnant women, and is also used as a sweetener in sugar-free products.

Note: Manna ash gum may irritate sensitive skins.

Towards meditation

Manna ash is the obvious choice today because the first Office reading recounts the story of the Children of Israel being fed manna in the wilderness. Once again, the Old Testament (here Wisdom 10, referring to 'the food of angels') foreshadows the New Testament, in that through Christ we receive the true Bread from heaven, in the form of Blessed Sacrament and written Word. But the manna ash has scented flowers and its gum is sweet, and this recalls another of today's themes. In the second Office reading, St Augustine tells us that 'there is no scent more fragrant than that of the Lord. All who believe must possess this perfume.' He is saying that the way to possess it is through sincere prayer. In the gospel Christ scathingly condemns those who lay burdens on others but do not practise what they preach and are full of hypocrisy and ostentation. The scented flowers of prayer will bloom only if offered in humility and self-effacement. These flowers are in fact greater closeness to God, and our practical demonstrations of love and care for one another.

Bible readings

Exodus 16:1–18: Manna in the wilderness.
Wisdom 16:20: The food of angels.
Isaiah 1:10, 16–20: If you are willing and obedient you shall eat the good things of the land.
James 2:14–18b: Faith and good works.
John 6:32: It is my Father who gives you the true bread.
Matthew 23:1–12: The greatest must be humble.

Intercessions

For greater depth, humility and sincerity in prayer.
   Thanksgiving for Word and Eucharist.

Place of spiritual retreat
In the crowds listening to Jesus teaching, as in Matthew 23.

WEDNESDAY WEEK TWO IN LENT

COMMON REED *Phragmites australis*
GOLDEN ROD *Solidago virgaurea*

Cultivation notes

The British native Giant Reed towers to a height of 10 feet and forms extensive reedbeds in fens, lakes and river margins. It flowers in July and August and has jointed stems and a creeping root system, which makes it invasive and difficult to eradicate. However, there are other more controllable grasses or sedges that will call to mind the same symbolism and are recommended in a domestic pond. A good one for a large pond margin, and also useful in dried arrangements, is the sweet galingale (*Cyperus longus*). It grows to about three feet, is still quite invasive, and will need vigilance. For a small pond try *C. vegetus*. This grows to between one and two feet. Sow seeds in spring or divide clumps in summer.

Golden rod is an attractive hardy perennial that grows to about four feet and produces masses of small golden yellow flowers from mid- to late summer. It likes well-drained, moist soil and a position in sun or part shade. Divide plants in autumn and spring. Golden rod attracts lacewings and ladybirds so is a good defence in the battle against aphids.

History and lore

The reeds referred to in the Bible are either *Anundo donax*, which can grow to eighteen feet and is common along the Jordan valley (see 2 Kings 18.21), or *Phragmites*, which was used for making pens (see Ezek. 9:2; 3 John 13). This is found in marshes in many parts of the Holy Land (see 2 Macc. 4:20; Jer. 36:23). A reed was a standard measure of six cubits (eight to nine feet), and we know that parts of the temple were measured by 'reed' (see Ezek. 42:15–20). The name *phragmites* is thought to come from the Greek *phragma*, meaning fence, screen or enclosure, and indeed stems may be used for these purposes. Our primitive ancestors probably built rough, temporary shelters with it, and in Britain reeds have been traditionally used for thatching in areas where they abound. They provide raw material for matting and fibre for the textile and paper industries, and they are used in flood-control schemes. The roots, shoots and seeds are edible, and the stems contain a sweet gum that was used as sugar substitute by Native North Americans. Nowadays they are used to make a sweet, cooling sedative. They are diuretic and said to be good for controlling the effects of food-poisoning, especially from seafoods. In Britain they provide a wonderful habitat for wild life, notably the reed-warbler, which uses their leaves and stems to build light, safe and bulky nests.

Several species of golden rod are common in North America, where they have a long history of medicinal use by indigenous tribes. In Britain they grow wild in woods, on heaths and on rocky uplands. They are cultivated in gardens because of their long show of colour. Traditionally respected as a healer of internal complaints and external wounds, golden rod was much in demand during the sixteenth century, when it was applied in an ointment or drunk in a hot infusion. It was imported in large quantities and was very expensive until it was discovered growing wild on Hampstead Heath. *Solidago* derives from Latin *solidare*: to make whole or join. In modern herbalism, infusions of golden rod are used to treat arthritis and eczema and to relieve nausea. Powders of dried leaves are applied to ulcers. The parts used are the leaves and flowering tops before fully open.

Towards meditation

In today's first Office reading we are told of the people's thirst in the wilderness, of how they complained and found fault with Moses and 'murmured against him'. Turning to God in his dilemma he was told to strike the rock with his rod. This he did, and water gushed forth. But we are not meant to understand the event merely in literal terms of physical thirst being quenched. Yet again Moses is a type of Christ, whom we know as the very foundation of life, physical and spiritual. Even he, however, was the victim of murmurings, and the scribes and Pharisees refused to listen to him. St Irenaeus, in the second Office reading, enlightens us by showing how, through events that foreshadowed the future, Israel learned to fear God and to persevere in his service. 'He called them by temporal things to eternal things, by the carnal to the spiritual, by the earthly to the heavenly.' Irenaeus goes on to quote St Paul: 'For they drank from that spiritual rock which followed them; and the rock was Christ.' The responsory after the reading underlines the lesson, also from Paul: 'Until faith came, we were all being kept in bondage to the Law, waiting for the faith that was one day to be revealed.'

As for the reed, like us, it cannot survive or flourish without water (see Job 8:11), but today it holds another significance. The first Mass reading reminds us that Jeremiah, like Moses and many other prophets and patriarchs, was a victim of the obduracy of the people. 'Come let us smite him with the tongue; let us not heed any of his words.' In the case of Jesus they not only reviled him with their tongues before they crucified him but also smote him with the very reed they had given him to hold as the mock sceptre of the King of the Jews. But this is not the end, and with Paul we believe that, in the new covenant, the rod of Moses becomes the golden rod of the King of Glory, the means by which we may drink the water from the spiritual rock, and the reed becomes the sceptre of his universal rule under which we hope to live in eternal wonder, love and praise.

Bible readings
Exodus 17:1–16: Water from the rock.
Jeremiah 18:18–20: Come let us strike him.
Psalm 30:5–6: Save me in your love.
Galatians 3:23–5: The law was our teacher bringing us to Christ.
Matthew 20:17–28: They will condemn him to death.

Intercessions
For all who work in the stationery, publishing and building industries, particularly those involved in the dissemination of the Word of God, and in the design of buildings for his worship; for thatchers and fence-makers.

For the victims of floods and those involved in schemes to prevent flooding, and to promote a fairer distribution of water in the world.

For insomniacs and victims of food-poisoning; for workers in wildlife preservation; for sufferers from arthritis and eczema and ulcers.

Place of spiritual retreat
Pondering Jesus' teaching with the disciples, as in Matthew 20.

THURSDAY WEEK TWO IN LENT

ALDER *Alnus glutinosa*

Cultivation notes
This deciduous bushy shrub has regular branches that make a conical

shape. It flowers in early spring and produces catkins in the autumn. The male catkins are longer than the female, which resemble small cones. After the fruit has ripened in October, the tree remains green almost until leaf-fall. It favours moist to wet soil, sun and partial shade, and in these conditions can grow up to 70 feet. The bark is purplish to grey. Alder has the rare ability to turn nitrogen from the air into valuable plant food; nodules on the roots contain bacteria that fix the nitrogen, which makes up for the lack of it in wet soil. Plant to enrich poor soil or prevent erosion.

History and lore

The alder extends over the whole of Europe into Siberia, the Caucasus and Asia Minor, and is believed to have been in Britain for at least 8,000 years. It is the tree of our fens, swamps, lakes and riversides. The name comes from Anglo-Saxon *aler*. Alder wood is whitish-yellow when felled, but with exposure to the air it becomes brick-red and then paler in colour as the wood dries. This led to the belief that evil lurked in the tree and the old German legend of the malign *Erlkönig* comes to mind, as does Schubert's intense and chilling *Lied* of that name. It is often translated as 'Elf-king', but, strictly speaking, it should be 'Alder-king'.

Alder wood is easily worked. Sixteenth-century Venice is supposed to have been built on alder piles, and the wood has traditionally been used for making dishes, spoons, canoe paddles, cradles, clogs, mouldings, window-frames and pencils. It has also been employed in the manufacture of gunpowder and in the salmon-smoking industry. It takes paint and polish well. The bark and leaves produce an astringent tonic that encourages the healing of damaged tissue and is also good for rheumatism. The leaves can be used in poultices: gather the leaves in summer and use fresh. The dye from alder bark is black: peel the bark from 2–3-year-old trees.

Towards meditation

The alder is chosen because of its preference for water, and because in today's liturgy water represents the willingness of God to love and nourish those who love and fear him. Jeremiah contrasts the person who ignores God with the one who seeks him: 'He is like a shrub in the desert and shall not see any good come', compared with 'He is like a tree planted by water that sends out its roots by the stream and does not fear when heat comes for its leaves remain green and it is not anxious in the year of drought, for it does not cease to bear fruit.' This is virtually repeated in the responsorial psalm at Mass. The gospel is the parable of Dives and Lazarus, which Christ preached to the Pharisees, tax-collectors and sinners. Dives, who lived richly but ignored the law and the prophets, is in hell, whereas Lazarus, who was a beggar but a good man during his life, is in 'Abraham's bosom'. Dives' anguished request for water to cool his tongue is refused, and he is told that there is no chance of his ever getting out of his place of torment. When he asks that someone be sent from the dead to warn his brothers of their own impending fate, he is told that they too have already been warned by the scriptures and have paid no heed. The parable ends prophetically: 'If they do not hear Moses and the prophets, neither will they be convinced if someone should rise from the dead.' In the second Office reading St Hilary underlines the importance of listening now, the importance of being convinced by the One who rose from the dead, the importance of loving and fearing the Lord. We should take serious note of Jeremiah's comparison, and of the psalm; most of all we should heed the message of the gospel. We have been warned, and we should seek to become like the alder tree and draw strength, health, love and nourishment from the 'water' that is Christ himself.

Bible readings
Exodus 18:13–27: The Judges given office under Moses.
Deuteronomy 30:2–3a: The Lord will restore your fortunes.
Jeremiah 17:5–10: A blessing on the man who puts his trust in God.
Psalm 1: Happy the man who does not follow the counsel of the wicked.
Psalm 39: Happy the man who trusts God.
James 4:7–9: Wash your hands clean.
Luke 16:19–31: Dives and Lazarus.

Intercessions
For the peoples of countries where the alder is native; for Venice, its citizens and patriarch; for singers of German *Lieder*.

For carpenters and wood-carvers; for those in the dyeing and fish-smoking industries.

That we may seek God more nearly, and study and heed the scriptures.

Thanksgiving for God's love and for the 'One who rose from the dead'.

Place of spiritual retreat
With Our Lord as he deals with the Pharisees, as in Luke 16.

FRIDAY WEEK TWO IN LENT

VINEYARDS

Cultivation notes (See Thursday Week Four in Lent (p. 87) for further comment on the grapevine (*Vitis vinifera*).

The books will tell you that vines demand sun and a great deal of attention throughout the year, and that they should be planted outdoors running from north to south. However that may be, my French neighbour grows his few vines from east to west and always seems to have a good crop for the table and for making the local aperitif, *Pineau des Charentes*. This is commercially produced in vast quantities, but most households have a few vines for making their own.

History and lore

The grapevine is of great antiquity and occurs over the temperate and sub-tropical zones of the world north of the equator. *V. vinifera* was probably first cultivated more than 5,000 years ago, and viticulture was well developed under the ancient Egyptians. Wild vines are thought to have grown in Greece, Italy and France, but cultivated varieties were introduced by the Syrians, Phoenicians and Mesopotamians. Vineyards spread north through France under the Romans, and through Spain under the Carthaginians. The earliest known book on viticulture is Carthaginian, but it is known only in a Latin version, which in its turn is probably a translation from Greek. Grapevines had reached the Rhineland by the first century AD and southern England by the third. They were certainly there during the reign of the emperor Probus (235–82). Up to his time Italy had had the monopoly in wine-producing vineyards. Probus is supposed to have relaxed this grip and to have come to England and planted the first vine at The Vyne in Hampshire. He was eventually murdered by a mutinous army, whom he had set to drain marshes at Sirmium (in modern Kosovo). The decline of English viticulture was gradual between the Roman period and the time of the Domesday Book (1086) which records the existence of only 38 vineyards, almost a third of which were monastic. The largest, at Bisham Abbey in Berkshire, covered 12 acres. The English had not lost interest in growing the vine, or indeed in drinking its product, but the climate had become increasingly too cold to make it worth the effort. We had to wait until the twentieth century for improved conditions and a revival. Now there are over 420 wine-producing English vineyards covering almost 2,500 acres.

Towards meditation

It must be impossible for anyone who knows scripture to gaze on a vineyard without seeing and reflecting on its spiritual meanings. The Jews have a tradition that the first vine was planted by God on the fertile slopes of Hebron, and many texts in the Old Testament feature the vineyard as a symbol of the Jewish nation that God planted in Canaan. The Psalmist remembers this and asks God, 'Why then hast thou broken down its walls, so that all who pass along the way pluck its fruit? ... They have burned it with fire, they have cut it down.' He pleads with God to look down and see and protect the vine. But the prophets explain the reason for devastation. When God's people love, obey and follow him they bear fruit; if they turn from him and worship idols they become a 'ruined vineyard' and produce nothing. These facts will remain true as long as humans have a choice to make. The Israelites worshipped other gods, and so does Western society today. Our gods are money, technology, our own cleverness and our preoccupation with bodily beauty and carnal satisfaction. We too are a stiff-necked people. However, today's liturgy takes the symbolism of the vineyard even further: it sees it as not only the Israelite nation but as the whole world, and it is concerned with that world's rejection of God's Son. It finds prophecy of this in Isaiah and in Christ's parable of the vineyard, where the tenants throw out and kill the son of the owner. Here Christ prophesies his own death, and again we are warned of the fate of the throwers-out and the murderers. God, the owner of the vineyard, will lease it 'to other tenants who will give him the fruits in their seasons'. But there is still hope because 'by his knowledge shall the righteous one, my servant, make many to be accounted righteous; and he shall bear their iniquities' (Isa. 53:11); and the Psalmist also prophesies: 'The stone which the builders rejected has become the head of the corner. This is the Lord's doing; it is marvellous in our eyes (Ps. 118:22).

Bible readings

Genesis 37:3–28: Joseph's rejection prefigures the rejection of Christ.
1 Kings 12:28–9: No worshipping of other gods.
Isaiah 5:1–7: The ruined vineyard.
Ezekiel 15:1–8: Jerusalem the fruitless vineyard.

Isaiah 53: The Man of Sorrows.
Matthew 21:33–46: The parable of the owner of the vineyard.

Intercessions
Thanksgiving for the grapevine; for viticulturists and all who are economically dependent on their produce; for moderation in the consumption of wine; that more of God's people will turn to him from their worship of false gods.

Place of spiritual retreat
Amongst the Pharisees, tax-collectors and sinners listening to Christ's parable, as in Matthew 21.

SATURDAY WEEK TWO IN LENT

BALM OF GILEAD *Commiphora opobalsamum*

This rare desert shrub is the true 'balm of Gilead'. It was supposed to have been a gift to Solomon from the Queen of Sheba, and it is now protected and its export forbidden. However, there are two other plants commonly called 'balm of Gilead' that you can plant instead.

Cultivation notes
1. *Cedronella canariensis*: this attractive shrubby and semi-evergreen perennial is native to the Canary Isles and is called balm of Gilead because of the scent of its leaves. *Cedronella* is the diminutive of cedar and also refers to the plant's aroma. It produces spikes of tubular pink, violet, or lilac flowers in summer and can grow to a height of five feet. It is ornamental and aromatic, but has no therapeutic use. Grow in a 10-inch pot under cover or in a sunny position in the garden. Sow in spring and thin to 18 inches apart and take care because seedlings resemble those of nettles. Pick before flowering and then dry for pot-pourri.
2. *Populus balsamifera (P. candicans; P. x gileadensis)*: these ornamental hardy trees like deep, moist, well-drained soil and sun. Propagate in winter by hardwood cuttings. Prune hard before spring to encourage new foliage. Collect the sticky resinous buds in spring before they open and use for infusions. They contain salicin, the aspirin substance, and are widely used in cough mixtures and as inhalants to clear the sinuses. Infusions applied

to the skin can be antiseptic, relieve pain and improve blood circulation. An ointment made from the buds is good for cuts and bruises and as a general analgesic. The tree can grow to 80 feet if not checked. Avoid planting near buildings as the extensive and invasive root system can damage drains and foundations.

History and lore

On Holy (Maundy) Thursday as many priests as possible will gather with their bishops in the cathedrals of their dioceses for a service of great solemnity and beauty. During this Mass the blessing of the holy oils takes place. Afterwards each priest will take back to his parish enough of the oils for the sacramental needs of the coming year. St Basil attributes the origin of this practice to Apostolic tradition. From the beginning the blessing could be done only by patriarchs in the East and by bishops in the West, but for centuries it could be done on any day of the year. Then, in 845, Pope Leo wrote to the emperor from the Council of Meaux, fixing the day as Maundy Thursday. Three oils are blessed, but it is the oil of chrism that particularly interests me today. Chrism is distinguished from the other oils by having balm as an ingredient. It is the oil used to anoint the crown of the head at baptism. A *christom* was a white cloth laid by the priest on a newly baptized and anointed child. Shakespeare knew this. In *Henry V* (Act II, scene iii) he has Mistress Quickly tell us how Falstaff had died and 'made a finer end and went away an it had been any Christom child', that is, as innocently as a child still wearing the *christom*. Chrism is also applied to the foreheads of confirmands, and the bishop who administers it has also received it at his consecration.

The practice of mixing balm into the chrism dates from about the sixth century, originally from trees growing in Judea and Arabia, but since the sixteenth century the West Indies and other tropical countries have been the source of most ecclesiastical balm. In some eastern rites, up to as many as 40 different spices and perfumes are used in addition to balm. The olive oil in Chrism symbolizes the fullness of grace imparted through the sacraments, and the balm, that 'fragrant tear of dry bark', represents freedom from corruption and 'the good odour of Christ' – that is, of absolute virtue and sanctity. During the blessing of the chrism, the bishop blesses the balm and then mixes it with a little oil and prays that 'whosoever is outwardly anointed with this oil may be so anointed inwardly that he may be made a partaker of the heavenly kingdom'. The word 'Christ' itself means anointed one, and so through our receiving the

chrism at our baptism and confirmation, we are truly 'Christed' by one
who is 'Christed' himself.

Towards meditation

All the balms, including *Melissa* (see lemon balm; Monday Week Four in
Lent, p. 79), are associated with the easing of pain; with soothing
ointment; with peace, calm and comfort; with freedom from anxiety and
corruption; and with the preparation of bodies for the grave. These
associations chime with the Church's preoccupations today. The liturgy
takes us through the cycle of our knowing the law, of the grace poured out
upon us at baptism and confirmation; of our breaking the law and
impeding grace through our sins; of our turning to God in penitence and
desire for the balm of his forgiveness. In sin we are dead; in repentance
and forgiveness we come to life in Christ. The mystery of pain and
hardship remains, but the overriding atmosphere today is comforting. In
the first Mass reading Gilead is used as a symbol of the divine pity and
pardon that awaits us if we repent; the psalm speaks of God as a healer of
all ill, and as the one who overcomes the corruption of the grave; the law
given on Mount Sinai, like the New Law of Christ for us, is 'perfect and
revives the soul'. The gospel expresses the welcome that God has in store
for us if we return to him in penitence, sorrow and love. In the second
Office reading, which is an extract from the *Treatise on Flight from the World*
by St Ambrose of Milan, the importance of loyalty to God is underlined.
He it is who dwells in endless tranquillity. We should flee to him in our
minds, and in him we will find peace and rest from labour.

Bible readings

Exodus 20:1–17: The law given on Mount Sinai.
Isaiah 1:16–18: Wash; make yourselves clean.
Micah 7:14–15, 18–20: Shepherd thy people with thy staff.
Psalm 103: The Lord is merciful and gracious, slow to anger and
abounding in steadfast love.
Galatians 6:7–8: He who sows from the Spirit, will reap eternal life from
the Spirit.
2 Corinthians 6:1–10: Acceptance of hardship, punishment, misunder-
standing.
Luke 15:11–32: This your brother was dead and is alive.

Intercessions

For those in the therapeutic oils industry; for priests and bishops; for families and individuals preparing for baptism and confirmation that will take place during Eastertide.

Thanksgiving for our own baptism and confirmation, and for the sacrament of reconciliation; for our confessors.

For all who suffer in mind or body.

Place of spiritual retreat

With Jesus as he tells the parable of the Prodigal Son, as in Luke 15.

THIRD WEEK IN LENT

THIRD SUNDAY IN LENT

HART'S TONGUE FERN *Phyllitis scolopendrium*

Cultivation notes

This evergreen perennial is common in moist, shady places in the wild. Its wavy fronds can grow up to a foot long, and the plant itself to about 15 inches. There are several growing out of the masonry surrounding a drainpipe soakaway in a corner where our school building meets a boundary wall. Here the plants benefit from intermittent sunlight, and during heavy rain the guttering leaks above them, thus providing the perfect habitat. The plant can also be grown indoors and, as with many houseplants, its watering is a balancing act between underwatering and waterlogging. The compost must never be allowed to dry out, but over-wet soil will lead to rot. In any case, reduce watering in winter, provide indirect brightness, re-pot in spring, and keep the crown of the plant above compost-level.

History and lore

In Victorian times fern collections were extremely popular in conservatories, but very few were grown indoors, where fumes from gas-lamps and coal-fires were toxic to the plants. Central heating is kinder, but hot dry air is to be avoided. The fronds were once used to soothe scalds and burns, and Culpeper recommends it as 'a good remedy for the liver, both to strengthen it when weak, and to ease it when afflicted'. In modern herbalism it is still an ingredient in liver tonics, and will also ease sediment from the bladder. Topers take note!

Towards meditation

A moisture-loving plant is an obvious choice today since it is one of the Sundays on which the examination of catechumens may take place. The Mass introit draws attention to the promise God is about to fulfil: 'I will sprinkle clean water upon you, and you shall be clean from all your uncleannesses, and from all your idols I will cleanse you' (Ezek. 36:25).

The Old Testament reading reminds us of the occasion in the wilderness when the people, tormented by thirst, grumbled to Moses, who was then instructed by God to strike water from the rock at Massah and Meribah. Here God quenches physical thirst as a sign that he is with his flock, thus foreshadowing Jesus, who, in veiled language, will tell the Samaritan woman that the water he offers will eternally quench our spiritual thirst and bring us to everlasting life. In the second Office reading, from the pen of St Augustine of Hippo, we find a beautiful and cogent interpretation of the incident at the well. The woman, he writes, who came to believe after her encounter with Christ, is a symbol of the Church about to be born; moreover she is a foreigner, further symbolizing that the Church would come to and from the Gentiles. We must see ourselves in her. Like her we come in ignorant lack of understanding. When Jesus asks her, and therefore us, for water, his real thirst is for our faith. 'He is in need as one who will accept, he abounds as one who will satisfy.' The water he promised her, and now promises us, 'is plentiful nourishment and the abundant fullness of the Holy Spirit'.

And so the hart's tongue ferns at school lead me to a daily reflective gratitude for the water Christ gives us. As for today, it will not end without a meditative reading of Psalm 42, and wherever I am the words and tune of a favourite hymn will be replaying in my mind:

> As pants the hart for cooling streams
> When heated in the chase,
> So longs my soul, O God, for thee,
> And thy refreshing grace.[11]

Bible readings
Exodus 17:3–7: You must strike the rock and water will flow from it.
Psalm 42: As a hart longs for flowing streams.
Ezekiel 36:23–6: I will sprinkle you with clean water.
John 7:37–9: If anyone thirst, let him come to me and drink.
John 4:5–42: There came a woman of Samaria to draw water.

Intercessions
For sufferers from burns, and liver or bladder complaints; for those who live in areas of drought and water pollution.

Thanksgiving for our own water supply, and a promise not to be wasteful with it; thanksgiving for hymn-writers and composers throughout the ages.

Place of spiritual retreat
At the well with the woman of Samaria, as in John 4.

MONDAY WEEK THREE IN LENT

SAGE *Salvia officinalis*; *S. salvatrix* (sage the saviour)

Cultivation notes
This shrubby perennial is the common sage, producing purple, pink, or
violet flowers in summer and growing to a height of about 30 inches. I like
to have tricolour sage as well because it connotes the Holy Trinity, and for
a white/silver part of the garden I intend to try *S. officinalis* 'Albaflora'.
Propagate sage by softwood cuttings in spring and summer, or by division
in autumn or spring. It will become straggly and woody with age, and the
books all say it should be replaced every four to seven years. I have reason
to be grateful for its spreading habit. During the long exile from my
garden, described in the first book of this series, one of my sage bushes
grew so rampantly that it covered more than half the herbary. It was hard
work to get it under control again, but much more enjoyable than
grubbing up the forest of long-rooted nettles that would have held sway
but for sage, my green guardian.

History and lore
Salvia is from the Latin *salvare*, to be in good health, and the herb has long
signified immortality. The old Roman proverb has come down to us,
'How can a man die when he has sage in his garden?' And the old English
rhyme has it: 'He that would live for aye / Must eat sage in May.'
    Its reputation for encouraging longevity dates from the classical period,
and it has been grown in northern Europe since medieval times. It was
thought to grow best for the wise, which may be the reason for the English
name. Another English rhyme found in *The Englishman's Doctor* (1607)
neatly expresses the plant's folklore:

> In Latin salvia takes the name of safety,
> In English it is rather wise than craftie;
> Still the name betokens wise and saving,
> We count it nature's friend and worth the having.

The condition of the plant was believed to indicate the state of health in the household in whose garden it grew, and it was also regarded as a symbol of domestic virtue. For this reason it always reminds me of St Martha, the patron of housekeepers, who has been very good to me over the years, and to whom my vegetable-growing is affectionately dedicated each season.

It was also thought that sage alleviated grief, and it was scattered or planted on graves. Samuel Pepys wrote: 'Between Gosport and South-ampton we observed a little church where it was customary to sow all the graves with sage.'[12] Yet another tradition was that sage flourished where there was 'petticoat' rule. Margaret Baker, in *Folklore and Customs of Rural England*,[13] reports that as recently as 1948 a north-Oxfordshire man, fearing his neighbours' derision, chopped down a healthy sage bush for: 'If sage bush thrives and grows / The master's not the master and he knows.' And there is a Buckinghamshire saying that 'the wife rules when sage grows vigorously in the garden'. In France it is one of the ten Herbs of St John that are used to celebrate the Baptist's birthday on 24 June. The other nine are bracken, ground ivy, sundew, yarrow, marguerite, chamomile, mugwort, vervain and St John's wort.

Sage has many uses. For centuries it was employed more in the sick-room than in the kitchen. William Coles claimed: 'Sage helps the nerves, and, by its powerful might, / Palsies and Feavers sharp it puts to flight.' In a probable reference to Parkinson's disease, Andrew Borde wrote of its use in treating 'the sickness which doth make a mannes head to shake or the handes or other partes to quake'. It was also given to pregnant women and those wishing to be so. Introduced to North America in the seventeenth century, it grows wild there and was once listed as an official medicine in the United States Pharmocopia. The Chinese allegedly valued it so highly that they traded their finest teas for it.

Sage leaves are antiseptic and anti-fungal. They are also good for the liver and for the digestion, which is why we use it to accompany rich and fatty meats. In modern herbalism sage is used to combat depression, night-sweats and excessive salivation. Smoke from burning sage leaves is a good air-freshener, and the dried leaves discourage insects. Conversely, when flowering in the garden, the plant is attractive to bees. An infusion of fresh leaves makes a rinse that has a blonding effect on hair. To make sage tea, use tea and dried sage in equal parts, cover with boiling water, and leave to simmer for two hours. I find sage, together with rosemary, bay, thyme and eucalyptus attractive and versatile in wall and table decorations. I often place a herbal posy at the table setting of each dinner guest, and it is amazing what memories and stories these call forth during the meal.

Gather leaves for kitchen and dining-room at any time, but before flowering for any other purpose. Dry slowly for the best flavour. Hang in loose bunches in a dark, dry, warm environment. If a suitable outhouse is not available, the airing cupboard is a good substitute.

Note: Do not take large doses of sage over a long period of time. It is not now given in pregnancy, or, since it suppresses lactation, to nursing mothers. Do not give to epileptics.

Towards meditation

The lore and uses of sage offer several avenues for meditation, and each year I select a different one. First, as today's Mass readings remind us, Jesus was sent, like Elisha and Elijah before him, not to the Jews alone. The life he offers is the reward of all who yearn for it, for all who believe in him. Then, in the second Office reading St Basil writes about Christ's reversal of our death-sentence, whilst the responsory from Wisdom and John's Gospel says that to acknowledge God is perfect virtue and eternal life is in knowing Christ. Today then it would be appropriate to meditate on one of the Gospel accounts of Our Lord's passion and death, through which he wrought our *true* salvation and eternal life. A third theme is that of health, and this could lead to a meditation on the occasions when Jesus healed the sick. I could read about the man with the skin disease, the centurion's servant, Peter's mother-in-law, the paralytic. These healings demonstrate the power of Jesus over the whole range of human sickness. The most striking thing to me, however, is the strength and importance of faith in those involved, particularly in the case of the centurion, for whom it was not necessary to see Jesus cure his servant. For him, Jesus had only, and at a distance, to 'say but the word'.

The motif of domestic virtue could lead me to reflect on the account in Luke of Jesus' visit to the sisters at Bethany. Jesus does not tell Martha that her work is unnecessary, rather that she should not become so anxious about it as to forget the one thing really necessary, namely, to listen to the word of God and to contemplate his presence. I love this scene at Bethany because of its domesticity and, regardless of my affection for St Martha, because of its defence of the contemplative life. I have always had, particularly at this time of year, to be busy about practical matters, and when I am most under pressure I find this passage always calms me down.

It disperses anxiety and brings me back refreshed and energized by the true priority. If Jesus comes as my guest I must make sure that I have a spiritual 'table posy' for him. And I will most certainly re-read a favourite poem of Rumer Godden's, 'The House in Bethany'.[14] A few best-loved lines must suffice here:

> because it is no legend or old history:
> Bethany is my village, your town or street, everywhere.
> Martha's brisk plaits, the veil of Mary's hair,
> Both throw my shadow on the wall of the lighted sitting-room,
> Antagonists in every woman as everyday she makes her home:
> And Martha forever has no time to waste –
> Her tribute is the supper – Mary knows a richer feast.

Bible readings
Psalm 42: So longs my soul for thee, O God.
Wisdom 15:3: To know God is complete righteousness.
Luke 4:24–30: Jesus speaks of Naaman and Elisha.
Matthew 8:1–17: The man with skin disease.
Matthew 9:1–8: The paralytic cured.
Luke 10:36–42: Jesus visits Mary and Martha.
John 18 and 19: The passion and death of Jesus.

Intercessions
For the sick in mind and body; for couples who are unwillingly childless; for housekeepers; for members of religious orders, active and contemplative.

Thanksgiving for the life and work of Felicitas Corrigan and Rumer Godden; thanksgiving for health, if we are well; for strength, courage and endurance and healing if we are sick.

For courage, strength and energy to carry out our duties in life; for calm in which to pray; for an increase in faith and wisdom.

Places of spiritual retreat
At a chosen point in the Passion, as in John 18.
In the crowd as Jesus speaks of Elisha, as in Luke 4.
At the healing of the centurion's servant or in the house of Peter's mother-in-law, as in Matthew 8.
In the house at Bethany, as in Luke 10.

TUESDAY WEEK THREE IN LENT

SOAPWORT *Saponaria*; fuller's herb; bouncing Bet

Cultivation notes

Soapwort is a hardy perennial and can grow up to three feet in height. It likes damp and fairly shady conditions, self-seeds readily, and is potentially invasive. It has a family relationship with *Dianthus* and produces pale pink, clove-scented flowers, borne in clusters from mid-summer to mid-autumn. Cut back after flowering to induce a second crop of flowers. Soapwort is poisonous to fish and therefore should be kept away from ponds.

History and lore

Soapwort is thought to have been used as a cleaning agent by Assyrians in the eighth century BC. Pliny (AD 23–79) uses *saponis* for soap. My Latin dictionary says that *sapo* is a Celtic word. However, the Romans are believed to have used it as a water-softener, and it can still be found growing near the sites of old Roman baths. Saponin is the lathering substance, present in its highest concentration in the plant's roots. The leaves contain less, but when crushed will exude a liquid that provides a soothing face and hand wash for a hot and dirty gardener who does not wish to waste time going indoors to the bathroom. Soapwort was cultivated on the nineteenth-century herb farms of the American Shakers and now grows wild in fields and waste-places throughout the United States. In Switzerland sheep were dipped in a wash of soapwort to clean their fleeces before shearing. Before the commercial production of soap in the 1800s, soapwort was widely used for cleaning and there was a time when every cottager grew the plant for that purpose. It is apparently still in use in the Middle East. In Britain wild soapwort can suggest the site of old woollen mills because boiled leaves produce a mild detergent, which was once used for washing newly woven cloth. It was obviously put to similar use in France since there it is known as *herbe à foulon* (fuller's herb) and *saponière* (soap-provider). Richard Mabey[15] mentions it as growing wild on the small islands and banks of the River Don in Sheffield. Little did this author know of it as she journeyed through the Don valley to primary school in Pitsmoor in the early 1950s. Little then did she know either that Culpeper had claimed that soapwort was an absolute cure for syphilis, or that in 1931 Mrs Grieve in *A Modern Herbal*[16] had also recommended soapwort where mercury, the standard treatment of the disease for 400 years, had failed. Today it still provides a soothing wash for eczema, poison ivy rash, acne and psoriasis.

Soapwort is so gentle that it is still used in some museums and galleries for cleaning delicate furniture, upholstery, tapestries and pictures. This summer I intend to bring back some roots of soapwort to make a cleaning solution for the sacristan of our church to use on delicate church linen.

The leaves and stems should be harvested in summer, and the roots preferably in autumn. Dry the flowers and leaves; slice the roots and dry in the sun if possible.

Note: On no account should soapwort be taken internally; the root is particularly poisonous.

Towards meditation

In spite of its poisonous properties, I think of soapwort as a kind, gentle, merciful and soothing plant. Its character is in accord with today's liturgy, major themes of which are the cleansing, purging nature of effective Lenten practice; the need for humility, forgiveness and mercy; and God's mercy and forgiveness to us (which he will not extend to us unless we forgive each other).

The prayer of St Francis is a wonderful expression of this:

> Lord, make me an instrument of your peace: where there is hatred, let me sow love; where there is injury, pardon; where there is doubt, faith; where there is darkness, light; where there is despair, hope; and where there is sadness, joy. Divine master, grant that I may not so much seek to be consoled as to console; to be understood as to understand; to be loved as to love. For it is in giving that we receive, it is in pardoning that we are pardoned, and in dying that we are born to eternal life.

All our Lenten observance is useless unless we can do these things freely, without a struggle, and in love. In the garden, however, the root of soapwort also signifies the poisonous potential for cruelty in each one of us, while the cleansing, fragrant leaves, stems and flowers represent our calling to kindness, mercy and love.

Bible readings
Exodus 32:1–20: Israel's unfaithfulness.
Daniel 3:25, 33–43: May the contrite soul be acceptable to you.
Psalm 24: 4–9: Remember your mercy, Lord.
Psalm 156: Fasting allows preparation of the heart, cleansing of the flesh and a weeding out of vices.
Tobit 12:8–9: Prayer joined to fasting and almsgiving will purge away sin.
Matthew 18:21–35: Forgive your brother seventy times seven.

Intercessions
For sheep-farmers world-wide; for workers in the wool industry; for restorers of museum artefacts; for sacristans and vestment-makers; for needleworkers and machinists; for the people of Sheffield.

For those with acute and chronic skin disease; for sufferers from venereal disease.

For more kindness, forgiveness and mercy between Christians.

Place of spiritual retreat
With Peter listening to the parable of the debtor servant, as in Matthew 18.

WEDNESDAY WEEK THREE IN LENT

GREATER CELANDINE *Chelidonium majus*; swallow-wort; tetterwort

Cultivation notes
This hardy perennial is a member of the poppy family. It grows three feet in height, has greyish-green leaves, and produces yellow, four-petalled flowers from early summer. These are followed by capsules about two inches long, which contain the black seed. Celandine likes moist conditions in sun or shade. It self-seeds readily, so you are unlikely to need to propagate, either by sowing seed or by dividing roots in spring. It is naturalized in my woodland area and has to be kept under control. Fortunately it has a shallow root system and comes up easily. Ants eat the oil and carry away the seed. It is also popular in my garden with flat, red-

backed, geometrically black-marked insects the size of ladybirds, known locally as 'gendarmes' possibly because of their tendency to go round in attached pairs, the one appearing to push and the other to pull.

History and lore

The orange sap of celandine has been used since the early days of Chinese civilization for treating corns and warts. The name *tetterwort*, from Anglo-Saxon *teter*, used of a variety of skin eruptions, indicates similar use in the British Isles. In the first century BC, Dioscorides, who spent time as a surgeon with the Roman army, said that the name derived from *chelidon*, the Greek for swallow, perhaps because it is supposed to flower at the time when the swallows arrive. Pliny tells us that swallows discovered the plant and adds that the flowers fade when the swallows depart. Another tradition has it that mother swallows used celandine juice to restore the sight of blind nestlings. In England, *The Doctrine of Signatures* dictated its use in the treatment of liver disorders in humans and animals, particularly in dogs. This was because its colour resembled that of bile. The Revd C. A. Johns claims in *Flowers of the Field* that celandine sap had been successful in removing film from the cornea of the eye, and Deni Bown in her *Encyclopedia of Herbs*[17] reports its present-day use in the treatment of cataract.

Celandine sap can irritate sensitive skins and is poisonous, so in spite of its careful use in modern homeopathy it is best to avoid it in a domestic setting. The plant is naturalized in North America.

Towards meditation

The connection of celandine with warts cannot fail to remind me of Oliver Cromwell, who famously adjured his portraitist Mr Lely not to flatter but to paint truthfully what he saw: 'Remark all these roughnesses, pimples, warts ... Otherwise I will never pay a farthing for it.' 'Warts and all' is now a commonly understood idiom, the warts representing a person's foibles and peccadilloes. Any day in Lent is a good time to face up to our own, and today I will certainly spend some time acknowledging mine. Later I may consider the association of celandine with sight. The liturgy is at pains to point out that it is not enough to know the law, to be aware of the revelation God made of himself to Moses and brought to fullness in Jesus Christ. We must not only 'notice' but also 'observe', 'keep' and 'teach' this law and revelation in order to 'be considered great in the Kingdom of Heaven'.

In the second Office reading St Theophilus speaks of 'The vision of God'. God, he tells us, can be seen only when the eyes of our souls are opened. To a greater or lesser extent most of us have the cataracts of sin over our eyes. But God will cure the eyes of our souls and hearts if we recognize his power to heal through the Word. He has all power, all knowledge, all intelligence, all wisdom, with which he created the world and holds it in being. If we know these truths, we are privileged; if we live by them, we may see him. But we only begin in this if faith and fear of God are paramount in us. We will not understand what is necessary until this is true of us. We must do a thing almost impossibly difficult for us mortals, that is to 'put off what is mortal and put on imperishability'. Then we shall see God. 'For God raises up your flesh immortal with your soul; after becoming immortal you will then see the Immortal, if you believe in him now.'

Bible readings
Exodus 3:7–11: The full revelation of God made to Moses.
Deuteronomy 4:1–9: Take notice of the laws and observe them.
Matthew 5:17–19: The man who keeps these commandments and teaches them.

Intercessions
Thanksgiving for birds of the air and their song.

For sufferers from cataracts; for an end to pride and vanity; for greater faith, understanding, wisdom and fear of the Lord, that he will remove our 'cataracts' and help us to live his law and teach it, to do the thing we were made for, and yet because of sin can only do imperfectly.

Place of spiritual retreat
With the disciples as Jesus teaches them, as in Matthew 5.

THURSDAY WEEK THREE IN LENT

INCENSE PLANT *Humea elegans*
INCENSE CEDAR *Calocedrus decurens*

Cultivation notes

Humea is biennial and rightly classified as
elegant. When it grows well its long sprays of
small red-brown flowers can reach up to
six feet in height. The scent of incense comes
from the taller tough leaves. It is tender and
normally grown outdoors only in sub-tropical
conditions. In England and France therefore
a greenhouse is needed to raise it. Sow seed
from May to July in an unheated house. Pot on
seedlings singly. Move to larger pots as necessary
until by the following spring they will need ten-inch pots,
in which they will flower in summer. Shade may be necessary while the
flower-sprays are forming. Maintain a minimum temperature of 8°C
(45°F). It is important not to overwater and not to break the roots when
potting on.

The bright green, tight foliage of *Calocedrus decurens* forms a dense and
narrow column that can reach up to 115 feet if unchecked. The bark is
ridged and cinnamon coloured. It produces male and female flowers on
the same tree. The males are golden yellow, the females green, and it is
from the latter that the inch-long cones develop, with their scale-tips
turned outwards. The incense cedar does not mind shade but needs more
light with age.

History and lore

The incense cedar is in fact a member of the cypress family and its
common name comes from the fragrance of its foliage, wood and resin
when burned. The wood is finely grained but durable. The tree is a native
of Oregon and has been grown in Britain since 1853, when it was
introduced by The Oregon Association, a group of Scottish landowners. I
hope to plant a couple of the trees to fill gaps in my thuya hedge, and also
to offer one to the Commune for planting in the cemetery, where it would
symbolize our prayer for the dead buried there.

Incense is an ancient symbol of prayer and has been used down the centuries in the Orthodox and Roman Catholic liturgies. In the Church of England, although it fell into disuse after the Reformation, it never disappeared completely, and isolated places such as York Minster continued to burn it. Since the mid-nineteenth century and the coming of the Oxford Movement its use has become the norm in Anglo-Catholic churches. Biblical justification for incense in worship is not hard to find. In Exodus we have 'Take unto thee . . . the cleanest frankincense . . . And when thou hast beaten all into very small powder, thou shall set of it before the tabernacle. Most holy shall this incense be to you.' In Luke's account of the vision of Zachariah, the aged priest was 'offering incense in the temple of the Lord' just before he saw the angel who prophesied the birth of John the Baptist. The sacrificial worship of the Old Testament and its accompanying incense came to an end with the destruction of the Temple by the Romans in AD 70. The necessity for it had in any case been ended by the all-sufficient sacrifice of Christ. In Revelation we read of 'golden bowls of incense, which are the prayers of the saints'. John's account of his vision on Patmos is normally taken as symbolic, although looking around the world today one surely cannot be certain that it is absolutely so. Some authorities are of the opinion that John was strongly influenced by the liturgy of his own church. If so, we are like him when the burning of incense reminds us that our prayers ascend to the throne of God and join with the prayers of the saints in heaven. Like many other precious and valuable things we use at the altar, incense is a token of the best we have to offer, which in fact we are merely giving back to the One who created it.

Towards meditation
The choice of an incense-perfumed plant is clearly appropriate for a day when the liturgy concentrates on the necessity for, and the nature of, prayer. The first Office reading refers to the simple act of coming before God, while the scripture text at Morning Prayer pleads with God to listen to our supplication. The Old Testament reading and psalm at Mass speak of the listening aspect of prayer, and in the gospel Christ himself speaks of the prayer of action. (It is noteworthy that earlier in the chapter from which the gospel is taken, the disciples had asked Jesus to teach them to pray, and he had given them the Lord's Prayer.) At Prayer during the Day Isaiah enjoins us to 'call to the Lord while he is near'; at Evening Prayer James assures us that if we come close to God, he will come close to us; and the responsory to the second Office reading speaks of the nature of the worship and worshippers God really requires.

As is often the case it is the second Office reading that meditatively draws together and builds on the day's liturgical themes. Here we have Tertullian, from his *Treatise on Prayer*. Christian prayer, he says, is 'the spiritual offering which has abolished the ancient sacrifices'. God wants not burnt offerings but souls who will worship him in spirit and in truth: 'God is spirit, and so this is the kind of worshipper he wants.' The sacrifice he wants is 'one offered from the heart, fed on faith, prepared by truth, unblemished in innocence, pure in chastity, garlanded with love'. This we must offer to him together with good works and attendance at the liturgy. There is wise teaching here too on the efficacy of prayer in distress. 'It has no special grace to avert the experience of suffering, but it arms with endurance those who do suffer, who grieve, who are pained.'

Next, in a passage that will appeal to animal-lovers, Tertullian tells us that the whole creation prays. He maintains that the cattle and wild beasts come 'forth from their stalls and lairs, look up to heaven, their mouth not idle, making the spirit move in their own fashion'. The birds, he says, take flight heavenwards and 'spread out the cross of their wings' and in their song say 'something which may be supposed to be a prayer'. I do not find this fanciful, since every time we say the canticle from Daniel in the Office, which is frequently, we are praying that they should do just that:

> Bless the Lord, all birds of the air,
> Sing praise to him and highly exalt him for ever.
> Bless the Lord, all beasts and cattle,
> Sing praise to him and highly exalt him for ever ...

Tertullian concludes: 'Even the Lord himself prayed: to him be honour and power for ever and ever.'

Bible readings
Exodus 34:10–28: Three times a year shall your males appear before the Lord.
Psalm 142: Let my prayer be counted as incense before thee.
1 Kings 8:51–3a: Let thy eyes be open to the supplication of thy servant.
Isaiah 55:6–7: Seek the Lord while he may be found.
Jeremiah 7:25–8: They would not listen.
Psalm 95: O that today you would hearken to his voice.
Additions to Daniel 58–9: Bless the Lord.
James 4:7–8: Draw near to God and he will draw near to you.

John 4:23–4: True worshippers.
Luke 11:1–23: Lord teach us to pray.

Intercessions

For the departed; for those suffering pain or grief; for the poor and weak; for prisoners; for the rich; for travellers and wayfarers; for an end to persecution and theft.

Thanksgiving for the writings of the Fathers; thanksgiving for the birds and beasts.

For all of us sinners, the strength to resist temptation, the courage to stand for Christ and 'gather' with him, and the grace through prayer to become the kind of worshippers God wants.

Place of spiritual retreat

With Jesus and the disciples, as in Luke 11.

FRIDAY WEEK THREE IN LENT

PRICKLY MOSES ACACIA *Acacia farnesiana*

Cultivation notes

This deciduous fast-growing subject can be raised as a houseplant or in the garden as a hedge or small tree. It self-seeds readily, and where they are unwanted the results must be removed even before sapling stage, when they will have begun to develop a tough and spreading root system. The acacias were present when we bought our house and were identified for me by a French friend from the next village. The tree has sparse, feathery foliage stemming from larger branches and divided into between four and eight pairs of leaflets. The stems and branches are viciously thorny. The flowers, in the case of my trees, are a pale cream, and appear in late spring. When the petals fall they cover the herbary floor with a carpet of natural confetti. Three or four of them on the boundary of my land have grown into trees 12 feet in height. I have left them for two reasons: first, they grow behind the 'Calvary', and their thorns make them appropriate there; second, they add to the woodland appearance that the herbary seems to have taken on of its own accord – another thing I have decided to develop, rather than interfere and force it back to its original, traditional square beds for the herbs.

History and lore

Prickly Moses acacia is found in South-East Asia and is naturalized in Australia, where in some parts it is subject to control as a weed. The flowers are aromatic and contain insecticidal compounds. They are used in perfume and pot-pourri and can be added to bathwater to soften dry skin. The bark and pods yield a black dye. Harvest flowers as they open.

Towards meditation

The prickly Moses acacia is the 'thorn' in the title of the present book, and, representing as it does the passion of Our Lord, it becomes more significant the nearer we draw to Holy Week. Today it has other resonances. Moses is included in the tree's name possibly because its hard timber was used by the Israelites to build the ark and parts of the tabernacle. It is mentioned 11 times between Exodus 25:10 and 27:6. These thorny acacia trees were some of the few available in Sinai that were likely to produce pieces of sufficient length. So, in spite of my necessary strictness with their unwanted offspring, I am fond of my prickly acacias because of their biblical pedigree. They speak of the house of God, and this is a second reason that they are well placed on the northern boundary of my outdoor sanctuary. If the weather is kind I love to say the first Office today within view of them.

The first reading describes how and by whom, under instruction from Moses, God's requirements for the sanctuary and the ark were to be put into effect. In the responsory the Psalmist exclaims how lovely is God's dwelling-place, his soul longs for the courts of God, his heart and soul sing aloud for joy, for God is within that holy place. We as Christians read the Psalmist's words in two ways: first, he expresses how we feel about our own places of worship, our own tabernacle in our own sanctuary; second, we think of making our hearts and souls living tabernacles for God. But as today's liturgy unfolds, we remember that joy in God's presence is not the only reason we seek his courts. We go there to express sorrow for sin, and we know that unless we do so our souls will never be fit dwelling-places for him. In the words of Gregory the Great on 'the Sinless Sufferer', the second Office reading reminds us of the part played by our sins in making Christ suffer, and that the blood of our brother cries out from the ground.

Again and again, as the hours of the Office and the Mass unfold, we are enjoined to confess our sins, to come back to God, for he is merciful. Isaiah prophesies the saving, redeeming role of the innocent Christ, who himself in the gospel tells us what we must do to become fitting temples for him.

Bible readings
Exodus 35:30–36:1; 37:1–9: The building of the sanctuary.
Psalm 84: How lovely is your dwelling.
Isaiah 55:3: Incline your ear and come to me.
Genesis 4:10: The voice of your brother's blood is crying to me from the ground.
Isaiah 53:11b–12: The Righteous Servant shall make many righteous and shall bear their sins.
Hebrews 12:24: The blood of Jesus speaks more graciously than the blood of Abel.
Jeremiah 3:11–14: Return, O faithless children.
Mark 12:28–34: Love your neighbour.

Intercessions
For dyers and weavers; for carpenters, embroiderers and all who make church furnishings and artwork.

Thanksgiving for joy in the Lord and for our places of worship; for grace to live more perfectly the two great commandments of the New Covenant.

Place of spiritual retreat
With Jesus and the wise scribe, as in Mark 12.

SATURDAY WEEK THREE IN LENT

LOVAGE (LOVE PARSLEY) *Ligusticum officinales* (*L. levisticum*)

Cultivation notes
This hardy perennial has fleshy roots, hollow stems and smooth, divided leaves. Small yellow flowers appear in summer, followed by tiny seeds. It appreciates rich, moist soil in sun with some shade, and in favourable conditions it can grow up to six feet. Sow seed in autumn or plant in spring. Divide every few years. Love parsley produces new shoots early in the year when few other herbs are ready.

History and lore
Levisticum and 'lovage' come from the Latin *ligusticum* (Ligurian) because it once grew widely in Liguria. In medieval times it was known by the Old French *luvesche*. There was a custom of putting it in shoes to revive the feet of weary travellers, and it was served at wayside inns in a cordial that also contained tansy and a variety of yarrow known as *Achillea ligustica*. A modern version can be made by steeping lovage seeds in brandy. Sweeten with sugar (if wished) and drink to calm an upset stomach. Lovage has a strong celery-like flavour, so use with caution at first if you are unfamiliar with it. Young shoots are blanched and eaten as a vegetable; stalks are candied like angelica; the seed sprinkled on bread and cheese biscuits; and the leaves added to soups and casseroles. The oil is used in digestives, to treat poor appetite and to aid difficult labour. Lovage is sedative, aromatic, diuretic and expectorant. Harvest the leaves before flowering and dry for infusions. The seeds and three-year-old roots can also be dried and used in decoctions.

Towards meditation
Strictly speaking, lovage has nothing to do with love, but I have chosen it because of its English folk-name and because it is unflamboyant – the two themes of today's liturgy being love and humility. The latter virtue, according to St Francis de Sales, is the one from which all the others spring, including the love that God wants from us, that is, active and prayerful love, for him and for others. The second Office reading, from the addresses of St Gregory Nazianzen, is about serving Christ in the poor. Gregory refers us first to the Beatitudes and then to the fact that mercy is high on our Lord's list. My affectionate respect for St Gregory is deepened by this reading. He speaks of the need to give liberally, to be understanding and kind without demur or delay. We must not say to the needy, 'Come back later, I'm busy now.' Kindness, says Gregory, 'is the only thing that does not admit of delay'. Do your deeds of mercy with speed and cheerfulness immediately you perceive the need for them. Anything less falls short. In that regard Gregory presses home that we must throw out oppression, unfairness, meanness, scrutiny, ambiguity and grumbling. He goes on to exhort us all to take note of Matthew 25:34–40. Christ is the naked, the imprisoned, the starving, and we must clothe, visit and feed him. We may honour him at our table as Simon the leper did; we may anoint him with spikenard as Mary did; we may provide him with a grave as Joseph of Arimathea did; assist spiritually at his burial as

Nicodemus physically did; we may bring him our equivalents of gold, frankincense and myrrh; but if there is no compassion for his poor and little ones then it is all useless. He wants our kindness and compassion towards them. Unless we give them, there is no hope for us. Lord, grant us the grace to give, and love without stint, and with St Gregory I say, 'To you be glory for ever.'

Bible readings
Hosea 5:15–6:6: What I want is love not sacrifice.
Psalm 51: A broken and contrite heart you will not despise.
Isaiah 1:16: Help the oppressed, be just to the orphan, plead for the widow.
Matthew 25: When I was hungry you fed me.
John 15:12: Love one another as I have loved you.
Luke 18:9–14: The Pharisee and the tax-collector.

Intercessions
For workers in the perfume industry; for women in labour; for greater humility and love.

Place of spiritual retreat
With those who thought themselves righteous and despised others, listening to Christ's parable, as in Luke 18.

FOURTH WEEK IN LENT

FOURTH SUNDAY IN LENT
(Laetare/Refreshment/Mothering Sunday)

SWEET VIOLET *Viola odorata*

Cultivation notes

Violets are perennial and grow to a height of from four to six inches. They
like moist soil and a position where they will be in the sun either early or
late in the day, but not both. They produce runners that root every three
inches or so, and this makes them good for ground cover. The flowers
appear from late winter to mid-spring, and the heart-shaped leaves are
usually mid- to dark green. Plant in spring.

History and lore

The violet is found throughout temperate regions. It was commercially
grown as early as 400 BC in Greece, where it was made an emblem for
Athens. It has been associated with love and fertility since classical times
and was the flower of Aphrodite, the goddess of love, and later the Roman
Venus. The Romans are believed to have drunk violet wine, and were
criticized by Horace (65–8 BC) for growing fewer olives than violets. In
medieval times violets were strewn on floors in home and church to

sweeten the air and hide other smells. In English tradition they have acquired the meaning of sorrow and, paradoxically, of comfort, and they still signify shyness, modesty and innocence in the English mind. These meanings are hard to explain since the plant is supposed to have sprung from the blood of the boastful Ajax, and I have been unable to find the origin of the phrase 'shrinking violet'. It signifies innocence to Shakespeare, as he has Ophelia say after the death of Polonius that Hamlet, Gertrude and Claudius are all three unworthy of the emblem. Yet another symbolism is attached to the plant in the old lines: 'Violet is for faithfulnesse, / Which in me shall abide.'

Napoleon was nicknamed 'Corporal Violette', and died wearing a locket of violets taken from Josephine's grave. (She had worn violets at their wedding.) The violet achieved cult status in Victorian England and was grown on a vast scale for cut flowers and perfumery. It grows in great profusion in the American countryside and was made the state flower of Rhode Island in 1897, of Illinois in 1908 and of New Jersey in 1913.

The strange thing about the scent of violets is that it disappears once perceived, and for a while after sniffing violets one cannot smell anything at all. But hold the flower away for a minute or two and your olfactory sense will return. Perhaps this characteristic of the violet accounts for its popularity during the smellier periods of history.

Violets are still used, although not so widely as formerly, in the commercial production of breath-freshening sweets, and the oil is used in the manufacture of scent, toiletries and the liqueur *Parfait Amour*. A decoction of violet flowers makes an effective eyebath, or a mouthwash for ulcers. Petals can be crystallized for decorating puddings and cakes or, used judiciously, add sweetness and colour to confectionery. They can also be used as a garnish for salads or ices. Pick flowers when newly opened and the leaves in spring. Lift roots in autumn. All parts can be dried, but the flowers do not retain colour and perfume.

Note: High doses of violet may cause nausea and vomiting.

Traditions of the fourth Sunday in Lent

This Sunday, known as 'Laetare' because of the opening words of its Mass introit ('Rejoice Jerusalem'), offers a brief respite from the rigour and solemnity of Lent. In former times pink vestments were worn (as on 'Gaudete' Sunday in Advent), as a compromise between penitential purple and joyous white. 'Refreshment Sunday' is a term I have found more frequently used in the Anglican Church than in the Roman Catholic

Church. It may be explained by the fact that the gospel used to be John 6:1–15 (the Feeding of the Five Thousand), and it was acceptable on this day to eat simnel cake, indulge briefly in the things given up during the rest of Lent, and, as the Irish would say, 'have a good crack'. (The word 'simnel' comes, via Old French, from the Latin *siminellus* for fine bread, and *simila* for finest wheaten flour.) Nor was simnel cake the only delicacy – up and down the country other treats were enjoyed: in Hampshire, thin batter wafers; in Warwickshire, pork followed by fig pudding; and in Norfolk, a special plum pudding. But the universal country favourite was frumenty, prepared with wheat, milk and spices. There can be little doubt of the connection between all this feasting and Mothering Sunday. This name for the fourth Sunday in Lent is thought to have its origins in the ancient practice of visiting the 'mother church' or cathedral on this day, which in its turn possibly comes from Galatians 4:26, a verse from the former epistle of the Sunday: 'that Jerusalem which now is, and is in bondage with her children. But that Jerusalem which is above is free, which is our mother.' Perhaps the interpretation was that the present Jerusalem is the Church on earth, and the Jerusalem above our true home in heaven. Quite when it became the practice to go home to one's mother on this Sunday is lost in the mists of time, but certainly in the era of domestic service, apprenticeships, and of more children than now away at boarding school, it was common custom to obey the rhyme: 'On Mothering Sunday above all other,/Every child should dine with its mother.'

The holiday had somewhat declined by the outbreak of World War II, but American servicemen stationed in England helped to revive it by celebrating their own 'Mother's Day' on the second Sunday in May. The first such occasion was organized by a Miss Jarvis, who apparently was unaware of the customs of the old country. In France La fête des mères is celebrated on the last Sunday in May, so for five years my mother enjoyed two Mothering Sundays a year.

The visiting of mothers on this day never died out in my family, which is not surprising, since we have roots in Lancashire, a great simnel-eating county, and Cambridgeshire. Margaret Baker, in *Folklore and Customs of Rural England*, states that violets were the traditional offering, and indeed the first violets I remember were the ones my parents and I took to my grandmothers on Mothering Sunday in 1948, when I was four years old. In later childhood it became custom to collect pussy willow to go with the violets. I recall no discussion as to which flowers to take, and I am sure there wasn't one.

Violets they had to be, and violets they always were every year, until both grandmothers were dead and I began to give them to my own mother.

Towards meditation

I have chosen the violet because of its traditional connection with Mothering Sunday and my own memories, but also because its many connotations – love, fertility, sorrow, comfort, faithfulness, modesty, innocence – mean that it will always match at least one of the themes in the Mass cycle and be appropriate to Mary the Mother of Jesus and of us all. The introit tells those who mourn for Jerusalem to rejoice with her, and she is presented as a mother whose breasts give contentment and consolation. In 2 Chronicles 36 we hear of the wrath of God and the sorrow of exile experienced by his people, and then of his mercy, the cause of joy in release. In year two of the cycle we have Psalm 137, arguably the most heartrendingly beautiful song ever written in exile. Whatever the year I will read it today, and listen to Palestrina's setting, *Super flumina Babylonis*, which to my ear catches with painful poignancy, particularly on its last page, the yearning of the people for their homeland. In this music I hear wave upon wave of their lamentation. We too would be in eternal sorrow of exile from God because of sin, were it not for the fact that Christ has saved us and given us this cause for joy, as he tells Nicodemus in Chapter 3 of John's Gospel.

Mothering Sunday is a day for family reunion, brief feasting and fun, in which I partake wholeheartedly, but I know that, before the joy of Easter, Mary must meet her son on the road to Calvary and be present in the agony of the crucifixion, and for her, last summer, I pressed a maiden pink to keep between today's pages in my breviary.

Bible readings

Deuteronomy 2: Israel's wanderings.
Deuteronomy 4:29–31: Tribulation and return to God.
2 Chronicles 36:14–16: Exile and release.
Psalm 137: By the waters of Babylon we sat down and wept.
Isaiah 66:10–11: Rejoice with Jerusalem.
Nehemiah 8:9–10: This day is holy to the Lord, do not weep.
2 Corinthians 6:1–4a: Now is the day of salvation.
Ephesians 2:4–10: You were dead through sin and are saved through grace.
John 3:14–21: God sent his Son so that through him the world might be saved.

Intercessions
For those in love; for mothers; for exiles; for the grieving and sorrowful.
Thanksgiving for our mothers and grandmothers.
For the courage to be with Mary on the road to Calvary.

Place of spiritual retreat
With Christ and Nicodemus, as in John 3.

MONDAY WEEK FOUR IN LENT

LEMON BALM *Melissa officinalis*

Cultivation notes
This hardy herbaceous perennial can reach a height of three feet. It may
need controlling as it self-seeds readily and does not object to
transplantation. Clusters of unostentatious pale yellow flowers are
produced in summer. Lemon balm is a slow germinator and needs to be
sown in spring or planted in spring or autumn. It appreciates sun, but
likes shade at midday, and will grow in any moist, reasonable soil. Cut
back after flowering to encourage a fresh crop of leaves. Lemon balm is a
good companion plant to all crops, and there is a country tradition that it
promotes milk flow in cattle. It can be grown as a houseplant.

History and lore
It is almost certain that lemon balm originated in the Middle East, but it
spread quickly to the Mediterranean, where it has been cultivated for more
than 2,000 years, originally as a bee plant. *Melissa* is Greek for honey-bee.
In France, one of its country names is *piment des abeilles* (bee pepper), and
there is a tradition of rubbing the insides of hives with lemon balm to
prevent the inhabitants from 'vagabonding'. (I wonder if Brother Adam of
Buckfast followed this custom.) The Ancient Greeks used it as a medicine,
and the Roman Pliny wrote that 'they [bees] are delighted with this herb
above all others ... When they are straid away, they do finde their way
home again by it.' Paracelsus (1493–1541) called it the 'elixir of life' and
said that it would restore to new life anyone who took it; and John Evelyn
(1620–1706) claimed that it was 'sovereign for the brain, strengthening the
memory, and powerfully chasing away melancholy'. Indeed the ability of
lemon balm to lift depression has been famed for centuries, and it is still

used in aromatherapy for that purpose. The *London Dispensary* (1696) claims that if it be 'given every morning, it will renew youth, strengthen the brain, and relieve languishing nature'. Llewelyn, Prince of Glamorgan, a reputed centenarian, is supposed to have drunk balm tea every breakfast-time, whilst one John Hussey of Sydenham, after 50 years of the same practice, lived to 116 years of age. As for the ability of balm to aid memory, we find Thomas Cogan in *Haven of Health* (1584) commending to Oxford students a drink made from it: 'It is an herbe greatly to be esteemed of students ... for it driveth away heaviness of mind, sharpeneth the understanding, and encreaseth memory.' *Melissa* was probably at the height of its popularity during the Elizabethan period, and Shakespeare has his wracked Macbeth refer to sleep itself as 'Balm of hurt minds, great nature's second course, / Chief nourisher of life's feast'. Keats was later to claim, in *The Fall of Hyperion*, that a poet 'pours out a balm upon the world'. In the nineteenth century it was used to strew church pews, and in *The Language of Flowers* it signifies sympathy. And there is John Whittier's (1807–92) lovely hymn 'Dear Lord and Father of Mankind':

> Breathe through the heat of our desire
> Thy coolness and thy balm;
> Let sense be dumb, let flesh retire;
> Speak through the earthquake, wind and fire,
> O still small voice of calm!

Lemon balm was introduced to Britain from mainland Europe, certainly by the time Abbot Aelfric compiled his list of plants. In the present day it is naturalized in the south of England, and in the United States it grows wild by roads, woods and waste-places, from Maine to Kansas, and south to Florida and Arkansas. It can apparently also be found on the Pacific coast.

It is popular in herbal teas for calming the nervous system and is an ingredient in the French cordial *Eau de melisse des Carmes* (Carmelite melissa water), and in the liqueurs Benedictine and Chartreuse. Although leaves tend to lose their scent when dried, they can be added to pot-pourri or put into herbal pillows for their calming effect. The plant is a good insect-repellent, and the volatile oil is used in skin lotions. Fresh leaves are a soothing external treatment for gout and insect bites. I have found them more effective than dock when applied to nettle stings. In the kitchen, macerate the leaves in oil for a delicious lemony salad dressing. Harvest the leaves as flowering begins and handle gently to avoid bruising. Use the second crop of smaller leaves for drying. Hang bunches in a warm, dark, well-ventilated place, and then store in airtight containers in a cool, dark cupboard.

Towards meditation

Balm is chosen for two reasons. The first is its ability to lift melancholy. Today's liturgy reminds us that although we must go through our own sorrows and, more appositely, very soon now accompany our Lord in the worst sorrow of all, still in the words of the psalm (prophetic of Easter), 'Joy will come in the morning.' It is as if the Church knows that if she did not offer words of balm now, our spirits might fail in the face of the horror to come: 'I will rejoice and be glad for thy steadfast love, because thou hast seen my affliction.' The Psalmist of the Mass introit may have been speaking of his own affliction, and we may do so too at other times of the year, or when we are in personal turmoil, but today we can only think of the affliction Christ bore on our behalf, of his joy and of our joy in the salvation he has wrought for us. The first Mass reading is from Isaiah and uses imagery of earthly comfort, felicity and security to foretell the New Jerusalem, the Kingdom of Heaven, the opening of whose gates we shall very soon be celebrating. The whole point of our lives is to pass between them into the place where there will be no more weeping.

The second reason for the choice of lemon balm today is Paracelsus's claim that it 'would restore new life'. Tellingly, the gospel is the account of Christ's curing the son of the official at Capernaum (John 4:46–53). It has often occurred to me that surely all his healing miracles and his raisings from the dead are symbolic as well as actual. He means us to see that not only can he cure the whole range of human sickness, as Lord of Nature, but that through him alone can we be healed spiritually and made worthy of heaven; only through him can we be raised from the dead, not to a restoration of earthly life but to heavenly life eternal. And of paramount importance, as the father in the gospel demonstrates, is that we should have faith in these things.

Bible readings

Psalm 31:7–8: I will rejoice and be glad in thy steadfast love.
Psalm 30: I will extol thee, O God, for thou has drawn me up; weeping may tarry for the night, but joy comes in the morning.
Isaiah 65:17–21: Be glad and rejoice forever; no more shall be heard the sound of weeping.
John 4:45–54: Go, your son will live.

Intercessions

For dairy-farmers, beekeepers, and those involved in commercial honey production; for the depressed and sad; for university students; for Benedictines and Carmelites worldwide.

Thanksgiving for the writings of the poets and hymn-writers, particularly Shakespeare, Keats and Whittier; thanksgiving for the strengthening and positive nature of today's liturgy.

For an increase in faith, and the grace to go forward to the sorrow and pain of coming days, in the sure knowledge of Easter joy awaiting us.

Place of spiritual retreat

With Jesus and the official from Capernaum, as in John 4.

TUESDAY WEEK FOUR IN LENT

CRACK WILLOW *Salix fragilis*

Cultivation notes

In common with all willows, the crack willow loves water. Perhaps the least elegant among members of the *Salix* family native to Britain, it still has much to recommend it. The names 'crack' and *fragilis* come from the fact that its twigs are very brittle and snap off easily. In the natural setting of a riverside these then float downstream, lodge themselves in mud, and grow into new trees. This is fortuitous, as the seed of crack willow is short lived and requires moist soil to germinate. The tree is a fast grower, but tends to split if left to its own devices. It is often encouraged on river banks to prevent soil erosion with its long, deeply penetrating roots. In this environment the trees are usually pollarded to stop them splitting and to allow sun and air on to the river water. The practice produces sprawling and twisted specimens, but the crowns are so full of holes that they become home to leaf mould, which encourages the development of seedlings of other trees within them. According to Richard Mabey's *Flora Britannica*, ash, holly, gooseberry, elder, ferns, honeysuckle and brambles have all been identified in this habitat. He reports that Anita Jo Dunn examined 400 willow pollards on the river banks of west Oxfordshire and found 74 species growing in their crowns.

History and lore

In view of the brittle nature of crack willow twigs it is a paradox that the charcoal they produce breaks less easily than most other kinds and therefore is frequently preferred by artists. The roots produce a purple dye, and in some parts of Britain were traditionally used for painting eggs at Easter. Richard Mabey also reminds us that these trees formed the backdrop to Kenneth Grahame's *The Wind in the Willows* and inspired Arthur Rackham's illustrations and 'no slow river seems right without them now'. He goes on to describe how wands from pollarded willows will root immediately and make a natural fence. He repeats a story of this being done in Northamptonshire some years ago, appropriately by a Mr Pollard, whose grandson still lives nearby and so can appreciate the ingenuity of his grandfather.

Towards meditation

Two things inspire the choice of crack willow as today's plant. The first is its connection with fences and therefore with neighbours. Before my English neighbour acquired his cockerel and hens there was no need of a fence around the sides of my garden, which was then open to their depredations. Until then I was at one with Robert Frost in 'Mending Wall', where he mischievously wants to challenge his neighbour's ancestral adage, 'Good fences make good neighbours':

> *Why* do they make good neighbours? Isn't it
> Where there are cows? But here there are not cows.
> Before I built a wall I'd ask to know
> What I was walling in or walling out.[18]

Although I have not built a wall, I have been forced to put up a fence, and that will be protection enough. My French neighbour on the other side approves of the new fence. Since my return three years ago the boundary between us has become the regular scene of gardeners' chat, and the generous handing-over of edible produce on his part. He has witnessed my struggle over the years and must appreciate again having a garden instead of a weed factory next to his vegetables. After 14 years I think he has just about accepted me as a serious gardener. Meanwhile in London my neighbour, Carmen, looks after bulbs and houseplants in my absence and does all sorts of other things. I am truly blessed in my neighbours, and considering them today offers much food for meditation.

My second reason for choosing crack willow is its association with water. The Church continues to comfort us today, and this time it is with the life-sustaining water that features strongly in the texts at Mass. We take metaphorically that water which was literally vital to the wandering Children of Israel. When we read the introit we think of the thirst it describes as a spiritual one that can only be quenched by Christ. In the first reading Ezekiel tells of his seeing water issuing from below the threshold of the temple. It is a long and inspiring reading and one does not want it to end. The prophet is taken along the banks of the river and told wonderful things about it: 'On both sides of the river, there will grow all kinds of trees for food. Their leaves will not wither nor their fruit fail ... because the water for them flows from the sanctuary / Their fruit will be for food, and their leaves for healing.' The Mass psalm mentions a river whose streams make glad the City of God. Yet again the Spirit uses a thing essential to life, clean, sparkling and beautiful in itself, to show to our finite minds something of the infinite beauty of the City of God. We will encounter this image again during Eastertide, when for many days the Office looks at the Revelation of St John on Patmos.

Today's gospel is another account of healing, but here water is involved negatively. A man is healed by a pool that has a reputation for cures when its waters are disturbed. He tells our Lord that he can never get there in time. He is cured near the water but not by it; he is cured by Christ. Perhaps the message here is that Christ is able to cure without earthly agents or symbols, as he does on this occasion. Elsewhere he mixes spittle with mud to restore sight, perhaps so that the blind man could feel his touch, and perhaps so that the sighted could truly see. And perhaps we are meant to see from this cure at the pool that the old traditional places of healing are impotent and irrelevant in the face of the power of Christ.

Bible readings
Isaiah 55:1: Everyone who thirsts, come to the waters.
Ezekiel 47:1–12: Water was issuing from below the threshold of the temple.
Psalm 45: There is a river whose streams make glad the city of God.
John 5:1–16: There is in Jerusalem by the Sheep Gate a pool.

Intercessions
For the guardians of our river banks; for our close neighbours; for exiles.
Thanksgiving for the writers and illustrators who enchanted our childhood; for the poetry of Robert Frost.

For recognition of Christ's healing power; for increased joy and faith in the coming of the new Jerusalem.

Place of spiritual retreat
At the pool called Beth-zatha, as in John 5.

WEDNESDAY WEEK FOUR IN LENT

CUCUMBER *Cucumis sativa*
MELON *Cucumis melo*

Cultivation notes

According to Sutton and Sons, in *The Culture of Vegetables and Flowers*, 'a very small house, with an efficient heating apparatus, will suffice to provide a large and constant supply, and therefore winter cucumbers need not be regarded as beyond the range of practice of any ordinary well-kept garden'. However, a heated greenhouse is unnecessary for ridge cucumbers, which can be sown in a cold house in late April for planting out in June, or sown in the open in late May.

Melon-growing is another ball game altogether. The fruit are reared in much the same way as cucumbers but require firmer soil, higher temperature, stronger light, less water and more air. Sutton and Sons again, this time waxing metaphorical as well as didactic: 'No man should attempt to grow melons until he has some experience in growing cucumbers', which is 'a good practical preparation for the higher walk wherein melon is to be found'. Half a dozen plants should provide enough fruit for an average family, and indeed this number would be more than enough for the average gardener to cope with. Sow in a heated house (17°C, 65°F) between March and July, or in a cold house from May to September, bearing in mind that it will be four or five months before harvest. The earliest they can be ready is mid-August. Even in the south, growing melons in the open garden is a risk in Britain. In our region of France rows of hanging netted melons are a common summer sight, and obviously they are the small, sweet, pink-fleshed Charentais type.

Ridge cucumber plants can be bought at the local market here, and in recent years have been the only practical choice as my long absences preclude a greenhouse or growing from seed. These ridge cucumbers are prolific and their fruit shorter and fatter than the shop-bought variety, and they are therefore more economical in a small household. As for melons, I will not attempt them until we retire permanently to France.

History and lore

The cucumber is mentioned twice in the Bible. In Isaiah 1:8 we have 'as a lodge in a cucumber field'. The translation is probably inaccurate, as scholars believe the Hebrew *miqshah* really means 'the place of the water melon'. In Numbers 11:5, however, we have 'cucumbers and melons', so the intention seems to have been to refer to two distinct plants. The Hebrew for the first is *abattichim*, which probably means water melons, and for the second *qishshuin*, which may mean water melon, cucumber or gourd. All were known in ancient Egypt, and *cucumis sativa* was a popular salad plant. It is not surprising that the Israelites missed its thirst-quenching properties as they wandered in the wilderness.

The cucumber is native to India and has been grown there since ancient times; it was known to the Greeks and Romans and was probably brought to Britain by the latter. Long used as a cooling agent for the skin, it is popular nowadays in the form of pads to soothe tired eyes and in other herbal cosmetics.

Towards meditation

The liturgical theme of life-giving water continues today, and the complaints of the thirsty children of Israel and their memories of the good things of Egypt explain my choice of melon and cucumber. I could have selected leeks, onions or garlic, since their absence is also regretted in the first Office reading from Numbers, but somehow they do not have the same connotations of refreshment, restoration and consolation on which the rest of the day's liturgy concentrates. As usual, these gifts from God and signs of his love and mercy can be taken literally, but it is not long before we recognize a deeper meaning. This time water can be read as a symbol of God's mercy to those who repent of their sin. The second Office reading is from a letter of St Maximus the Confessor on that very theme, and its responsory includes the beautiful verse from Psalm 94: 'When the cares of my heart are many, thy consolations cheer my soul.' But water is also a symbol of the Holy Spirit, who even in Numbers is poured out on Joshua and the Elders. Joel prophesies that the Spirit will be poured out 'on all mankind'. And Christ himself promises that the ultimate and supreme Comforter will come to us on the morning of Pentecost. Whereas the strength of the Israelites was 'dried up', the Holy Spirit will work in us to the good, and we shall be filled with his power. In the gospel Our Lord explains the significance of his healing the man at the pool, and teaches us that 'as the Father raised the dead and gives them life, so the son gives life to whom he chooses'. And far from complaining about the things we miss or never had, it is this life in which we rejoice, and for which we thank him today.

Bible readings
Numbers 11:4–30: The people miss the fruits and vegetables of Egypt; the Spirit is poured out on Joshua.
Psalm 94:19: When cares are many thy consolations cheer my soul.
Isaiah 49:8–15: God promises to restore the land and to guide the people to springs of water.
Joel 2:28: I will pour out my spirit on all flesh.
Acts 1:8: You shall receive power when the Holy Spirit has come upon you.
Philippians 2:12b–15a: God is at work in you.
John 5:17–30: The Father raises the dead and gives them life; the Son gives life to whom he will.

Intercessions
For those dying of physical thirst; for those dying of spiritual thirst.

Thanksgiving for water and thirst-quenching plants; thanksgiving for the mercy of God, and for the comfort, strength and life given to us by the Holy Spirit.

Place of spiritual retreat
Listening to Jesus explain his cure of the man at the pool of Beth-zatha, as in John 5.

THURSDAY WEEK FOUR IN LENT

GRAPEVINE *Vitis vinifera*

Cultivation notes
Ordinary English gardeners normally have to grow grapes for the table under glass. In our part of France almost everyone grows a row of vines outdoors, mostly trained on post and wire, but some houses are fortunate

enough to have one climbing an exterior south-facing wall. There is a healthy specimen three doors up from us. Like the melon, the grapevine is for me a thing of the future, when I hope to be in permanent residence and thus able to give the year-round attention it requires. When the time comes I will take advice from an experienced neighbour, as anyone should who has not grown vines before. In England, a popular white grape for wine-making is Müller Thurgau, also widely available in France. Popular in our district is the paler Madeleine Angevine, and some November, soon, I hope for the gift of a few 'long cuttings' from next door.

History and lore
(See under Friday Week Two of Lent, p. 50.)

Towards meditation
As was noted some days ago, the vine can be seen as a symbol of the Jewish nation. Today, however, it has a different significance. In the first Office reading, the cluster of grapes from the country to which the people would not go up can be seen as a type of Christ himself. In the gospel he remonstrates with them because of their refusal to recognize him, even though they purport to believe in Moses, 'and Moses wrote of me'. Like the land flowing with milk and honey (see Deut. 1:25–32), he, as the true vine of the Kingdom of God, is also rejected. In his teaching Jesus makes frequent use of plants that were not only familiar to his hearers but also essential to their diet and way of life.

But there is a much deeper, more far-reaching significance in his choice of the vine to represent himself, and all the living and dead who are united to him as the living head, and who belong to every age, country, class and denomination. The Revd Hugh Macmillan muses on its aptness in *Bible Teaching in Nature*,[19] and since, so far as I know, the book is long out of print, I offer the following parapharase:

> This sacred vine is a unity and Christ is not the trunk or branches, but the whole vine. We are members of that vine, of his body, flesh and bone. This vine is immortal and has gone on increasing since the dawn of time; it will go on enlarging until all the redeemed have been grafted to it and it covers the whole of creation. Generations of Christians pass away as the annual shoots of the vine die, but the invisible Church endures, as the vine itself endures . . .

The vine is a most graceful plant, but its beauty is not ostentatious. It does not produce flamboyant flowers, but its foliage is graceful, its blossom fragrant, and its fruit exquisite in form. In this respect too, it is appropriate as an emblem of Christ, and of what we as his people hope to become, namely the perfect fruit of the Perfect Vine that is unutterably lovely, offering among the poison trees and thorns of sin a smooth stem, protective foliage and refreshing fruit. Through the Christian community and its individual members, the life of Christ has the potential to influence society. Were it not for this the world would 'speedily relapse into a howling moral wilderness' ...

Our union with Christ must be vital and productive for, 'every branch of mine that bears not fruit ... he takes away', but uprooting or cutting away is different from pruning, and 'every branch that does bear fruit he prunes, that it may bear more fruit ... Abide in me, and I in you. As the branch cannot bear fruit by itself unless it abides in the vine, neither can you, unless you abide in me. I am the vine, you are the branches. He who abides in me, and I in him, he it is that bears much fruit, for apart from me you can do nothing' (John 15:2–5).

Today therefore provides an opportunity to examine one's own condition in relation to the Sacred Vine, and to pray for the grace to bear fruit by prayer and action.

Bible readings
Exodus 32:7–14: Moses pleads for the people.
Numbers 12:16–13:3, 17–39: They came to Eshcol and cut down a single cluster of grapes.
Deuteronomy 1:25–32: It is a good land, yet you refused to go up.
Mark 12:1–10: A man planted a vineyard.
John 15:1–26: Jesus the true Vine and the Father the vinedresser.
John 5:31–47: If you believed Moses you would believe me, for he wrote of me.

Intercessions
For viticulturalists world-wide.
   Thanksgiving for the vine and its fruit; thanksgiving for the Sacred

Vine and his fruits; for wisdom to know whether we are being pruned or in danger of being uprooted, and for grace to take appropriate action.

Place of spiritual retreat
Listening to the words of Jesus, as in John 5 and 15.

FRIDAY WEEK FOUR IN LENT

VERONICA *Veronica filiformis (officinalis)*; speedwell
VERONICA *Hebe cupressoides; H. speciosa gloriosa*

Cultivation notes
V. filiformis is normally classed as a perennial lawn weed, rooting from small sections of stem. It is, however, the prettiest of weeds, and if you allow it to get a hold it will form mats of blue in spring. Certainly I do not need to cultivate it deliberately! It is with me and, even if I tried, it is doubtful I would ever eliminate it. In any case it already grows along the strip that will eventually be my pleached Way of the Cross, and I have already begun to rear masses of chamomile to join the speedwell in carpeting it. I plan vines to climb the uprights, and at ground level a selection of low-growing plants featured in this book.

Hebe is a tender subject and does best where it can be protected from frost. *H. cupressoides* grows to a height of five feet and produces pale blue flowers in June; *H. speciosa gloriosa* is even more tender, also grows to five feet in favourable conditions, and produces its pink or mauve flowers in July.

History and lore
In *The Language of Flowers* speedwell represents female fidelity, which is hardly surprising in view of the late medieval legend that on the road to Calvary a woman of Jerusalem wiped the face of Jesus with her head-cloth, and that the image of his face was then miraculously imprinted upon it. It is generally thought that the woman became known as Veronica from *vera icon*, that is 'true likeness'. The common name speedwell comes from the expression 'Godspeed', in the sense of a farewell, and may also refer to the fact that the flowers fade rapidly if picked. At any rate the women of Jerusalem were among the last to speak to Jesus before his crucifixion. *V. officinalis* was a popular herb during the Middle

Ages under the name *Herba veronica majoris*. In the nineteenth century it was favoured as a substitute for tea, to such an extent that in France it became known as '*le thé de l'Europe*'. So the little speedwell had its culinary use once, even though it is now generally despised.

In the early days of the Church many people made pilgrimages to the Holy Places in Jerusalem. The journey was arduous and the whole enterprise extremely dangerous, particularly after Jerusalem fell to the Sultans of Islam. And so the idea of performing the Stations of the Cross in churches came about. The Blessed Alvarez, a Dominican of Córdoba, is said to have built several chapels, each containing a representation of the different stages of Christ's sufferings. About 1350, the Franciscans, who had taken charge of the Holy Sepulchre, began to erect Stations in many of their European churches so that those who could not make the physical journey to Jerusalem might follow the Way of the Cross in spirit. Above each Station in church there should be a small cross. These are the true Stations; the reliefs and statuary that appear below them are not essential, and are there to help a deeper awareness of Christ's anguish and the magnitude of our debt to him. The hymn 'Stabat Mater', which often intersperses the Stations in public observance of the devotion, is said to be the work of a thirteenth-century disciple of St Francis, although it is inserted in the works of St Bernard in a manuscript at Utrecht.

Towards meditation

Today's liturgy is full of reference to the passion and death of Jesus. In the first Office reading, Moses, as a type of Christ, is murmured against by the people for whom he intercedes. This is exactly what will happen to Jesus, with the difference that his intercession and suffering have infinite power. At Mass the Old Testament reading from the book of Wisdom describes the errors and malice of the ungodly, and it is also prophetic of the treatment that will be meted out to our Lord. 'He is inconvenient to us', they say, 'and opposes our actions. He calls himself a child of God ... and boasts that God is his father ... let us see what will happen at the end of his life ... let us test him with insult and torture ... let us condemn him to a shameful death.' This is followed by undeserved words of comfort from Psalm 34: 'The face of the Lord is against evildoers ... the Lord is near to the broken-hearted and saves the crushed in spirit.' Jesus has been close to these throughout his earthly ministry, close to the widow of Nain, close to Jairus and close to Martha and Mary, who otherwise would have lost their only son, daughter and brother. On the terrible journey to Calvary he turns his face to the women of Jerusalem and, according to tradition, to his own mother. The second Office reading is from the Easter letters of Athanasius (c. 296–373) and speaks of the way in which through the Easter mystery those who are separated in the body are made spiritually close 'by the unity of faith'. The responsory of the reading combines prophecies of Zephaniah and of Christ himself: 'Wait for me says the Lord, for the day when I arise ... I shall draw all men to myself, when I am lifted up from the earth.' Morning Prayer revisits the prophecy of Isaiah concerning the manner of Christ's passion and its atoning purpose and efficacy. In the Mass gospel Jesus is in Galilee. Judea is not safe, 'because the Jews sought to kill him'. He goes up to the Feast of Tabernacles in private; there is much gossip and questioning among the people, who are well aware that the intention of the Jewish authorities is to kill him. In the face of this he preaches in the temple and again claims knowledge of the Father, 'for I have come from him and he sent me'. The atmosphere of menace continues to build: Jesus' arrest can only be a question of time, but *he* is in control of that time. Were it not so they would have arrested him in the temple there and then, 'but no one laid a hand on him, because his hour had not yet come'.

We know that soon our Lord will stand before Pilate and be condemned to death. And so today I begin to focus on the details of the road to Calvary. For many years I have followed the Stations every Saturday of Lent, either privately or in the company of fellow Christians in church. However, the devotion is so powerful that in recent times I have found that, starting today, it is helpful to concentrate on one Station per day, trying to enter into its mystery as deeply as possible and integrating that concentration into my prayer and participation in the liturgy as the remaining days of Lent unfold. This plan means that the fourteenth Station will be meditated on Maundy Thursday, and I have found that after this fortnight's preparation the full Stations made on Good Friday morning are more concentrated. For today then let us remain awhile at the first Station: Jesus is condemned to death.

Bible readings

Isaiah 53: He shall bear their iniquities.
Wisdom of Solomon 2:1, 12–22: Let us condemn him to a shameful death.
Psalm 34: The Lord is near to the broken-hearted and saves the crushed in spirit.

John 12:32: And I, when I am lifted up, will draw all men to myself.
John 7:1–30: They sought to arrest him; but no one laid hands on him.

Intercessions
For bereavement counsellors; for the broken-hearted and crushed in spirit, that Christ may send them his Spirit of comfort.

Thanksgiving for those who introduced the devotion of the Way of the Cross to the Church, for Jacopone da Todi's 'Stabat Mater', and for the music of many composers who have set it to music, particularly Pergolesi and Rossini.

For all Christian women, particularly those in religious life.

For courage to follow Jesus on the road to the Cross, that each of us may offer him our tiny crumb of comfort when we look into his face.

Place of spiritual retreat
Listening to Jesus teaching, as in John 7.

SATURDAY WEEK FOUR IN LENT

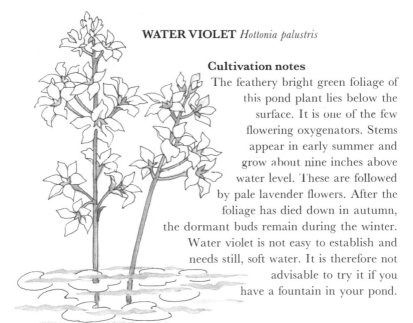

WATER VIOLET *Hottonia palustris*

Cultivation notes
The feathery bright green foliage of this pond plant lies below the surface. It is one of the few flowering oxygenators. Stems appear in early summer and grow about nine inches above water level. These are followed by pale lavender flowers. After the foliage has died down in autumn, the dormant buds remain during the winter. Water violet is not easy to establish and needs still, soft water. It is therefore not advisable to try it if you have a fountain in your pond.

History and lore

The species is named after Peter Hotton (1648–1709), Professor of Botany at Leiden University. *Palustris* is Latin for marsh or pond. An American variety, *H. inflata*, grows from Maine to Florida.

Towards meditation

The water violet is a suitable choice today because the events described in the first Office reading take place by the waters of Meribah. After Moses has struck water from the rock to satisfy the thirst of the people, they again set out, but it is not long before they complain again, this time because there is no food. God sends biting serpents, and then, under his instruction, Moses raises a bronze serpent on a pole. All who are bitten and who then look at the serpent are saved from death, thus foreshadowing the fact that believers in Jesus Christ raised on a cross are redeemed and promised life eternal. But I have also chosen the water violet because of its growth habit, appearance and symbolism. In religious art, the ordinary violet often represents humility, and Christ was 'humbler yet, even unto death, death on a cross'; the water violet is innocent and unassuming – Christ was as innocent and gentle as a lamb going for slaughter; it is not expected that a water plant should flower – it is expected that the Messiah will come from Bethlehem and not from Galilee, and therefore the uninformed, thinking that Jesus hails from Galilee, assume that he cannot possibly be that Messiah; the leaves of the water violet are hidden under water – the true provenance of Jesus seems at this point to be deliberately hidden from the Pharisees and the people. The feverish questioning of yesterday continues, and no answer is given. Moreover, it is Nicodemus who attempts to speak up for Christ among his fellow Pharisees – Nicodemus who has earlier sought Jesus under cover of darkness, for fear that his semi-discipleship may be discovered. Today's gospel ends with his round dismissal by his colleagues, 'Are you from Galilee too? Search and you will see that no prophet is to rise from Galilee.'

Following the plan begun yesterday, my concentration in the evening, either in church, at home, or in the garden, will be on the second Station: Jesus receives the cross.

Bible readings

Numbers 20:1–13; 21:4–9: At the waters of Meribah.
John 3:14–17: The Son of Man must be lifted up as Moses lifted up the serpent.

2 Corinthians 5:15: He died for all, that they might live for him who for their sake died and was raised.

Romans 4:25: He was put to death for our trespasses and raised for our justification.

John 3:1–21: Now there was a man of the Pharisees named Nicodemus.

John 7:40–52: Nicodemus argues with the Pharisees.

Intercessions

That we may look at the Cross, believe, and be saved; for grace more nearly to follow Christ's example of humility, innocence and gentleness; that we may fearlessly speak up for Christ, and not keep our allegiance under cover of darkness but openly proclaim it.

Place of spiritual retreat

With Nicodemus, as he visits Christ, as in John 3.

FIFTH WEEK IN LENT

FIFTH SUNDAY IN LENT

WHEAT *Triticum aestivum*; *T. compositum*
MAIZE *Zea mays*; sweet corn

Cultivation notes

Wheat is featured in today's gospel, but, since the ordinary gardener cannot grow it, I have included another popular cereal plant to remind us of it and to lead us into meditation. Grow sweet corn in blocks rather than rows, as this aids pollination. Drills should be 15 inches apart and three seeds sown at 12-inch intervals. Sow 1 inch deep under glass in mid-April, or without protection in mid-May. Thin at the five-leaf stage, taking out the two weaker plants. (I tend to buy market plants in June because my long absences from the garden preclude raising from seed.) Water frequently in dry weather and feed with a weak liquid manure once a week. Pinch off basal shoots when they are 6 inches long to strengthen the main stem. Weed regularly by hand and earth up for better rooting and support against wind. Up to 8 inches of stem can be covered in this way. Male flowers grow at the top of the stems and fertilize the lower female cob-forming flowers by dropping pollen onto them. In July assist the process by gently tapping the stems. When the cobs start to develop allow only three per plant, except on the most robust ones. After the silky tassels have withered in August, test for ripeness by stabbing one of the grains on the cob with a penknife. A milky juice indicates that the cob is ready and should be harvested and cooked as soon as possible for best flavour.

History and lore

The word 'corn' is confusing. In the United States it means maize or Indian corn, whilst in Britain it is a general word for the grain of all cereal plants, coming from the Teutonic *korno* via Anglo-Saxon. Our Corn Laws (repealed in 1846), the old Corn Exchange buildings in many towns and several of our hymns bear witness to this general usage. For instance: 'Fair waved the golden corn in Canaan's pleasant land / When full of joy, some

96

shining morn went forth the reaper band'; and 'First the grain and then the ear / Then the full corn shall appear.'

In the Bible 12 different words are used for wheat, depending on plant part and stage of growth. Nevertheless, it is reasonably certain that the wheat referred to is either *T. aestivum* or *T. compositum*. The latter may have seven ears on each stalk and is depicted in Egyptian hieroglyphics. The origins of *T. aestivum* (common bread wheat) have only recently been discovered, and it is now known to be an extremely ancient hybrid. As for maize, I can best convey its provenance by quoting the Revd Macmillan in *Bible Teaching in Nature* (1878): 'Maize spreads over an immense geographical area in the new World, where it has been known from time immemorial, and formed a principal element of that Indian civilisation which surprised the Spanish in Mexico and Peru.'

Bread, whether made from wheat, maize or other cereals, is still the main food of humankind, still the 'staff of life'. The staff was the ancient sceptre, and therefore the word suggests power, authority and dignity. It is refreshing to remember this when saying Psalm 23: 'Thy rod and thy staff they comfort me.' But the staff was also the central tent pole of nomadic peoples, and so to put down one's staff means to pitch camp or take up residence in a place. Where the staff is placed, the tent spreads and cannot be held up without it, much as life cannot be supported without bread. And so Jonathan Swift, in *The Tale of a Tub*,[20] says, 'Bread ... is the staff of life.' Nowadays of course bread is a metaphor for all food and, in slang, even for the money earned to buy it. In Christian language, 'the breaking of bread' is synonymous with Holy Communion and is often used when Christians share an ordinary meal together.

Towards meditation

It is no accident that our Lord used the symbols of wheat and bread in his teaching ministry, his prayer and his institution of the Eucharist. Literally, with water, bread is essential to life, and as the water of the Spirit gives us access to grace, so the Bread of Christ himself is essential to our spiritual life and hope of rising with him.

As a child I spent many fascinated hours watching and learning as my maternal grandmother made bread. Many years later I learned that her marriage to my charming and dapper grandfather was unhappy. Like my other grandmother, she had reasons for being miserable, but my happiest memories of her are of watching that bread-making. The lines of hurt etched into her face were smoothed away, and she appeared content, even serene. When I came to make bread in my own home, in times of sorrow and joy, I understood why this may have been: to be able to make the staple of our diet, in the warm kitchen fragrant with the activity, gives a sense of security. I think her momentary serenity came from the fact that bread-making made her forget the gnawing anguish inflicted by her errant husband. Bread-making will not and should not be hurried, and the dough must be thoroughly kneaded, 'proved' and shaped. It is a process that demands calm and patience. Impatient people cannot make good bread. The spiritual point does not need to be laboured.

It is in the botanical nature of wheat that one grain gives rise to several new ears, while the original is used up. In today's gospel, Christ takes this characteristic to show that spiritual fruitfulness has its origin in the death of self. But in this, his last public statement, when the Greeks came in search of him, he is staring at his own destiny: one that is full of paradox. He will buy eternal life for us with his own earthly death; he will achieve glory through the ignominy of the cross; and in his body, which must die, is his imminent rising. And so as I put dough to prove and rise in its place of warmth, I think of this as the tomb and the dough as all of us. As the dough is proved and shaped, so must we be 'proved' and spiritually shaped and stretched by God. And as the yeast causes the bread to rise, so we too may rise from sin and death to glory if we have the leaven of Christ thoroughly integrated within us.

Turning to reflect on the third Station, 'Jesus falls the first time under the weight of the cross', I reflect that, just as he metaphorically fell to earth as a grain of wheat at his Incarnation, so now he literally falls to it as the same grain that will die and yield a rich harvest.

Bible readings
Jeremiah 31:31–4: Deep within them I will plant my law.
Hebrews 5:7–9: He learned to obey and became the source of eternal salvation.
Hebrews 12:2: Christ Jesus is the radiant light of the Father's glory ... sustaining the universe.
1 Peter 4:13–14: Share in the sufferings of Christ.
1 Peter 5:10–11: You are called to eternal glory.
John 12:20–3: If a grain of wheat dies, it yields a rich harvest.

Intercessions

For cereal farmers and bakers world-wide; thanksgiving for our daily bread, physical and spiritual; renewed prayer that the resources of the earth may be more fairly distributed.

Thanksgiving for the lives and sacrifice of our grandmothers, and for the things they taught us to love and appreciate.

Thanksgiving for Christ's saving death and resurrection.

Place of spiritual retreat

Listening to Christ's words, as in John 12.

MONDAY WEEK FIVE IN LENT

RUE *Ruta graveolens*; herb of grace; herb of repentance

Cultivation notes

Rue is a perennial semi-evergreen sub-shrub with blue-grey leaves. Its small yellow flowers are strangely cupped and appear in loose clusters from June to September. Plant in September or March, or sow in spring. (Rue is a slow germinator.) Prune in spring and again in late summer to encourage new growth. Rue reaches a height of about two feet, enjoys full sun and light shade, and can be grown indoors. Protect in severe winters. Do not attempt to grow rue near basil. They do not like each other and inhibit each other's well-being.

History and lore

Ruta may derive from the Greek *rhutos*, meaning 'shielded', and indeed the herb has a long history as a remedial agent. It is thought to have been an ingredient in King Mithradates' all-purpose antidote, and in classical mythology Mercury gave Ulysses a sprig of rue to counteract the evil enchantment of Circe. It was valued in 'the old religion' as a mystical herb against witches and wrongdoing and has already been noted as one of the herbs of St John used to celebrate the Baptist's birthday. This tradition is probably another example of transmutation of a pagan feast into a Christian one, John's feast being the nearest in the calendar to midsummer's eve to warrant special honour.

Our Lord mentions rue in one of his castigations of the Pharisees (Luke 11:42). To be absolutely certain of obeying the law, they demanded that tithes be paid from the herb garden, even though the Talmud tithe rules applied only to agricultural produce. Many herbs were not even gardened as such, and if they simply sprang up they may even have been regarded as weeds. In any case Jesus could have been talking about wild rue, and this would certainly add force to his point in drawing attention to the pharisaic lack of a sense of proportion. *R. chalapensis* and *R. graveolens* still grow in the Holy Land.

At least since Elizabethan times rue has been a symbol of regret and called the 'herb of grace' because grace and forgiveness follow repentance. At one time it was probably used with hyssop to sprinkle the congregation at the asperges or *Vidi aquam* before Mass. Culpeper called it the 'holy herb'. Rue was thought to be effective against the plague and was an ingredient in the medieval antiseptic 'four thieves vinegar'. Robbers of houses where people had died of plague would douse themselves in it. A solution of sage, mint, rosemary, wormwood, camphor, rue and vinegar was used for washing, and judges carried sprigs of rue at the assizes to ward off gaol-fever and other infections that might be caught from the defendants who appeared before them. Rue has long been valued as beneficial to sight and as a remedy for tired eyes. Both Michelangelo and Leonardo da Vinci claimed it helped their natural and creative vision, and the flowers are still used in eye-lotions. The plant is shown on the heraldic emblem of the Order of the Thistle, and is supposed to have inspired the design of clubs in playing cards. It contains rutin, which is thought to strengthen teeth and bones, and rue tea is prescribed for nervous headaches and dizziness. (To make a cup of rue tea, infuse a teaspoon of rue leaves in boiling water for five minutes. Strain, and then to counteract the extreme bitterness add at least one tablespoon of honey.) Rue juice brings fast relief from the pain of wasp and bee stings. The plant is a good insect repellent and if rubbed into the fur of pets can deter fleas. This could explain its popularity as a strewing herb in medieval times. The best time to harvest leaves for drying is just before the flowers open, but it can be done from spring to early summer.

Note: Rue should not be taken in pregancy and can irritate sensitive skins.

Towards meditation

Milton knew all about the reputation of rue for soothing tired eyes and for clearing vision. In *Paradise Lost* (Book XI) the Archangel Michael, sent by God to show Adam a vision of the future, removes the film from his eyes,

> Which that false fruit that promised clearer sight
> Had bred; then purged with euphrasy and rue
> The visual nerve, for he had much to see;
> And from the well of life three drops instilled.

Michael had to use two powerful herbs to rectify the damage done to Adam's vision by his eating the forbidden fruit. Both euphrasy (eyebright) and rue are mentioned in Gerard's *Herball* as being restorative of sight, but there were many others. It is possible that Milton tried them all in the fight against his own blindness, and I believe his choice of these two for Michael's use was probably deliberate, both symbolically and doctrinally. Euphrasy is from the Greek word for cheerfulness, and the bitter rue is a pun on sorrow and repentance. The chosen herbs therefore relate to the joy and sorrow that Michael has already (in Book II) cautioned Adam to temper. But the adjustment to Adam's sight is connected with the workings of the 'well of life'. The grace to see aright and to repent spring from that well, and forgiveness depends on that grace: 'For with thee is the fountain of life; in thy light do we see light' (Psalm 36:9).

The poem is a vast word-painting of the truths enshrined in the liturgy of this penitential day, one of the most important being stressed in the second Office reading, from St John Fisher on Psalm 129: 'Even if someone has sinned, we have an advocate with the Father.' Returning to the Way of the Cross, we find at the fourth Station 'the author of our salvation' meeting with his mother on the road to Calvary. Here the connection of rue with sorrow is most poignant. The Man of Sorrows meets the Mother of Sorrows, and I commit to their care all who are in mourning and anguish.

Bible readings
Ezekiel 33:10–11a: Our sins weigh heavily upon us.
Jeremiah 31:2–4a: A humbled and contrite heart you will not spurn.
Romans 5:8–10: Christ died for us while we were yet sinners.
Hebrews 2:5–18: Jesus is the author of our salvation.
John 8:1–11: If there is one of you without sin, let him cast the first stone.

Intercessions
For a sense of proportion in the interpretation of the rules of religion; that we may be sensible and generous in the amount we give to support our churches; for grace to see aright and be truly repentant.

For those accused of crimes, guilty or not; for judges and officers of the law; for those with infectious diseases; for the blind and partially-sighted.

Thanksgiving for the life and work of artists and poets, particularly of Leonardo da Vinci, Michelangelo and John Milton.

Thanksgiving for our 'Advocate with the Father'.

Place of spiritual retreat
Listening to Christ's words, as in John 8.

TUESDAY WEEK FIVE IN LENT

HAZEL *Corylus avellana*; filbert; cobnut

Cultivation notes
Strictly speaking, hazel is not a tree but a bush, with branches growing straight from the ground. It reaches a height of up to 15 feet and is often self-sterile. The male flowers or catkins appear in February, and the female flowers are tiny buds with minute protruding red tassels. In the absence of these, or another self-fertile hazel growing nearby, you will not harvest any nuts. If the female flowers are present, the males will shower pollen on them and the resulting nuts ripen in autumn in clusters of two or three. Each one is held in place by a green, jagged, toothed husk, which turns brown as an indication that gathering should commence. Unless this comes away easily the nuts are not ready to eat.

History and lore
Together with the birch, hazel was one of the first plants to appear after the last Ice Age. The name is the modern form of the Anglo-Saxon *haesel*, possibly derived from *hase*, signifying the husk round each nut. Filbert is from St Philibert (c. 608–c. 685) on whose feast day (20 August) nuts were traditionally ripe. Cobnut is derived from a game of that name, cob meaning to throw gently. Players pitched a large nut at a pile of smaller ones. Those knocked from the pile became the property of the thrower. Hazel is common throughout Britain, Scandinavia and most of Europe. In the United States filberts are planted in the warmer parts, and a related species grows wild throughout the eastern states. In English tradition nuts are not gathered on Holy Cross Day (14 September) because that is when the devil goes a-nutting.

In English folklore the hazel is generally regarded as benevolent: Devonian brides were greeted by an old woman with a gift of hazelnuts for fertility; a good nut year still calls forth the remark, 'Plenty of nuts; plenty of cradles'; hazel branches were commonly used as cattle-droving sticks; in Yorkshire they were used as a charm for sheep at lambing time; and as recently as 1950 Somerset people stirred their jam with a hazel twig so that the fairies would not steal it. (Apparently it keeps jam from shrinking so there must be some chemical reason.) Tracing the sign of the Cross with a hazel twig on newly sown seedbeds was a common country practice, and, in Somerset again, a heart was often traced between two crosses. Another charm in May is to mark a cross with a hazel twig in the hearth ashes. In Britain and Europe hazel was invested with powers to protect from witches, venomous snakes and other evil dangers. Branches would be taken indoors to defend the house from lightning, the nuts were carried to relieve toothache and lumbago, and there is a legend that St Patrick drove the snakes out of Ireland with a hazel branch.

However much we may scoff at and dismiss these pagan rituals and beliefs, the hazel does possess one very mysterious property. In the process of water-divining it takes on a life of its own and completely controls the dowser. In the sixteenth century it was used to find mineral veins, and in Cornwall this finding power was attributed to the piskies. Vallemont (writing in the seventeenth century) called the hazel wand '*la baguette divinitoire*', and even mentions its use in the tracking and capture of criminals. Earlier, Roger Bacon had burned the wood for its charcoal and, with sulphur and saltpetre, made an early form of gunpowder.

Hazel-wood is white or reddish, soft and easy to cleave, although tough and flexible. Its rods are used in thatching and fencing, and formerly in wattle-and-daub building, a method thought to be at least 6,000 years old. The alleged first Christian church in England, at Glastonbury, was built in this way. In the garden, tall rods can be used as bean poles, or for staking tomatoes, whilst the smaller twigs can be used as pea-sticks. If you take rods for these purposes the bush will send up new shoots. In England the hazel is traditionally coppiced, that is, cut back to ground level for its rods every seventh year or so.

To make a hazel walking stick, or shepherd's crook, cut a rod in winter, selecting one that has the appropriate shape for a handle, and of a length suitable for the eventual user. Do not peel but leave to season for six months. When the process is complete the bark will come away easily. Shape the handle with a file and sandpaper, and then likewise the rest of the surfaces. Make several applications of furniture polish, buffing between each until the stick is coppery in colour. A really good crook would be a lovely gift for a bishop, or confessor, particularly since in *The Language of Flowers* the hazel symbolizes reconciliation. If the stick is for yourself, whenever you walk with it, let it remind you that Christ is our true reconciliation.

Towards meditation

The first of several reasons for choosing hazel today is its connection with snakes. The Old Testament reading at Mass is from Numbers and tells how God sends a plague of serpents among the people because they have spoken against him. When Moses intercedes for them, God tells him to make the fiery serpent and raise it on a standard so that those who are bitten and look at it will be saved. Second, the custom of making a sign of the Cross in the earth with a hazel twig reminds me that the serpent of Numbers is a type of the Cross of Christ, but whereas the Israelites had only to look at the serpent to stay alive on earth, we are brought to eternal life by Christ's death and resurrection. The second Office reading, from Pope St Leo the Great (d. 461), meditates on that Cross as the source of all blessings and the cause of all graces; in the Mass gospel Jesus refers to it himself: 'When you have lifted up the Son of Man, then you will know that I am he.' He has already made a similar allusion during the secret visit of Nicodemus in John 3, on that occasion referring directly to the Numbers incident. Hazel is also appropriate today because the many superstitions and false beliefs attaching to it, as well as its water-divining power, draw attention to our human tendency to be fascinated with mysterious things in an unbalanced way. There is an interesting episode in Hosea 4, where God says: 'My people enquire of a thing of wood, and their staff gives them oracles ... they have left their God to play the harlot.' This could be a reference to the hazel or to another tree with power to find hidden things. But God regards *reliance* on it as part of his people's apostasy. They relied on the thing itself and not on the One who gave it power.

Today's liturgy is full of comparisons and similarities. The faithfulness of Moses is compared with that of Christ, and both of these with the faithlessness of the Israelites, and later of the Pharisees. One cannot help but compare their apostasy with our own in modern times. The 'house' is not protected by the hazel branch but by Christ himself. He is faithful as the Son in charge of God's house, and we are his house. The whole building is bonded together not with hazel, wattle and daub, but by Christ, and in him grows into 'a holy temple in the Lord'.

Finally, I choose hazel because of its meaning of reconciliation and its famous mention in the writings of Julian of Norwich (1342–1416). In Chapter 5 of *Revelations of Divine Love*,[21] she is shown in her vision 'a little thing, the size of a hazelnut'. She marvels at its continued existence and then perceives that it is made by God who loves it and sustains its existence. But she is conscious that she can never know this God, can never find complete peace, rest and happiness until there is nothing whatsoever separating her from him. We will find these things not in trivia but in God himself, who is true rest. Pondering this passage from Julian, I humbly suppose her to be speaking of our eternal and complete reconciliation, towards which we constantly pray and work during our earthly lives.

Today I inspect my hazel, earmarking 'wands' to be cut in winter for making next year's crooks and walking sticks and, that done, will stay by it awhile to reflect on the fifth Station: Simon of Cyrene takes the cross from Jesus. As crooks and walking sticks support our weight, so Simon bears the instrument through which Christ will carry the weight of our sins. Through the Cross, that serpent of death whose sting is removed by our Saviour's hanging upon it, we are enabled to do Julian's bidding and renounce our apostate fondness for the trivia of the world and its false values, priorities and beliefs; through it we may find the peace, rest and happiness of which she speaks; through it we can be saved and truly reconciled. So although today inspires profound sorrow and repentance, it is also an occasion for unbounded joy and gratitude.

Bible reading
Numbers 21:4–9: If anyone looks at the fiery serpent, he shall live.
Hebrews 3:1–19: The faithfulness of Moses and of Christ.
Ephesians 2:20b–21: The whole structure is joined together in Jesus Christ.
John 3: There was a man of the Pharisees named Nicodemus.
John 8:21–30: When you have lifted up the Son of Man you will know that I am he.

Intercessions
For thatchers, fence-builders, and all who work with the wood or fruit of hazel.

Thanksgiving for the life and writings of Julian of Norwich.

That we my put our trust in Christ, our true future and reconciliation, rather than in the predictions of fortune tellers and the like; that our making the sign of the Cross over our seeds may be a prayer of dedication, and for their, and our, health and fruitfulness.

Place of spiritual retreat
With our Lord and Nicodemus, as in John 3, or listening to his self-identification, as in John 8.

WEDNESDAY WEEK FIVE IN LENT

FORGET-ME-NOT *Myosotis*; eyes of Mary; eyes of the infant Christ

Cultivation notes
This delicate and lovely little biennial should be sown in early summer, and transplanted when large enough to handle, for display the following spring. It likes moisture and partial shade and produces masses of small blue flowers. *M. sylvatica* has a yellow 'eye', grows to a height of up to 12 inches, and is often planted with tulips. Rock garden and edging types include *M. alpestris*, which has azure flowers and grows to eight inches, and *M. rupicola*, which is bright blue and minute at a maximum of two inches.

History and lore
In Victorian times, according to *The Language of Flowers*, if a man wished to declare love for a woman, he had to offer a bouquet of roses entwined with forget-me-not and lemon grass. In Germany it was the tradition to sow it on the graves of children, and strangely, in the spring following the Battle of Waterloo, the plant turned the devastated fields into a carpet of blue. I read somewhere once that forget-me-not juice was formerly believed to harden steel. This was a surprise, since even though I am a native Sheffielder I have never heard of such a thing and have so far been unable to find out anything more about the theory.

Forget-me-not is shortlived, and perhaps that explains its name, as if the plant is saying, 'I may not last long, but do not overlook me. Remember where you have planted me and my small beauty will enchant you again next year.' There is, however, an old legend that offers a charming explanation: as God was walking through the Garden of Eden in the cool of the evening after the Creation, he noticed a small blue flower, and asked if it knew its name. The plant, overcome with shyness, whispered that it was afraid it had forgotten. And God answered, 'It is Forget-me-not. And I will *not* forget you.'

Towards meditation

The constancy of God's love is a liturgical theme today and because of the legend I can think of no better plant to remind me of the fact that God never forgets us. Both Mass and Office invite us to reflect on the wonderful three-way relationship we have with God. He loves us, loves through us and is loved by us. As St Augustine says in the second Office reading, Jesus Christ prays for us, prays in us and is prayed by us. He does not forget us, and through our not forgetting him others are not forgotten. It is a day of consolation, and at this point in Lent it is well timed. In spite of the horror that we will commemorate next week, we can and must hold fast to our faith and our hope, remembering that the force and the purpose of it all was, is, and will be the love of God for us.

Returning to the Way of the Cross, we find Veronica at the sixth Station attempting to console Jesus, to ease his distress in a small way by wiping his face, and, whether or not Veronica existed, the Station ensures that we do not forget him, nor the need to imitate her legendary action in spirit. With St Thérèse of Lisieux we must seek to love him as he deserves to be loved. For as God loves and sustains Julian's hazelnut and the forget-me-nots that we plant, so he loves and sustains us And I have the feeling that if today at the sixth Station we recognize even a little of how truly amazing is the divine love shown for us in the sufferings and death of Christ, we shall each year be better prepared for Holy Week and its glorious aftermath.

Bible readings

Daniel 3:14–28: He has sent his angel to rescue his servants.
Hebrews 6:9–20: God does not forget us.
Hebrews 9:28: Those who have not forgotten him, he will not forget.
Ephesians 4:32–5:2: Order your lives in love.
John 16:2–23: The Father will give you anything in my name.

Intercessions

For florists; for those in love; for parents bereaved of children; and for families bereaved through war.

For those whose beauty is spiritual and unregarded.

Thanksgiving for the life and writings of St Thérèse of Lisieux; for the love that binds us to each other and to God.

That we may receive grace to glean from the liturgy the help we need to approach the coming week.

Place of spiritual retreat
Listening to Christ's instruction to ask of the Father, as in John 16.

THURSDAY WEEK FIVE IN LENT

FIG *Ficus carica*

Cultivation notes
The fig is deciduous and can grow up to more than 30 feet if not controlled. The imperfect flower is right in the centre of the 'fruit'. The gritty seeds are in fact the true fruits. The fig itself is really the seed-case. Some authorities favour fan-training against a south-facing wall or as a bush in a sunny corner. Figs need plenty of sun, and seldom suffer from pests or diseases. Mulch after planting and each April or May thereafter; begin feeding in late spring when the tree is four years old. The easiest thing about fig-growing is that most are now self-fertile. (They have to be because the British climate is not warm enough for the fig wasp that does the work of pollination in hot climates by entering the tree through tiny holes in the stalks.) If not controlled the roots of the tree will spread rampantly and produce plenty of foliage but no fruit. It may be preferable to grow the tree in a large pot and then plant the pot in what is traditionally known as a fig-pit, and from which it can be trained against a wall. If you use this method, although it is important never to let the roots dry out, there is the added advantage that the pot can be dug up and taken into a suitable outbuilding before frosts are expected. Repot every two to three years in late winter. March is the best time for initial planting of a two- to three-year-old tree. If your fig is left outdoors, give protection and do not remove this until the danger of frost is over. As soon as possible prepare netting to prevent theft by the birds and put this on as soon as the figs begin to form. If, despite your best efforts, there has been frost damage, now is the time to remove the affected branches. Top-dressing and cleaning up at soil level are important, as our Lord well knew (Luke 13:6–10).

The favourite, 'Brown Turkey', is still recommended for British gardens. It is hardy to –5°C, is ideal for pot-culture, but can grow to about 15 feet if not checked.

History and lore
Figs were a major crop in ancient Greece, where it became illegal to plunder or export them, and informers who reported infringements were known as sycophants from *sukon*, 'fig', and *phainein*, 'to show'. This linguistic history probably explains why the fruit came to signify flattery in English lore. The fig was important to the Israelites, and everyone liked to have his own fig tree as well as his own vine. 'Judah and Israel dwelt in safety ... every man under his vine and under his fig tree, all the days of Solomon' (1 Kings 4:25). Later God would use the vision of the baskets of good and bad figs to explain to Jeremiah that he was going to sort out the good from the bad in Judah (Jer. 24:1–10). In the Holy Land a well-cultivated specimen should produce fruit for ten months of the year and may live as long as 400 years. Not surprisingly, the fig tree also traditionally symbolizes proliferation. It was sacred to the Romans, who believed that it had sheltered the wolf that suckled Romulus and Remus, founders of their city. Pliny (AD 23–79) mentions 29 varieties. They were important as food and as medicine, the leaves being used to treat sore eyes and the milky sap from young figs to remove corns and warts. They remain effective as a gentle laxative and in the drawing of boils and abscesses. Simply split a fig, heat it and apply to the affected area. The treatment is particularly effective with gumboils.

The Romans are thought to have introduced the fig to Britain. Some authorities maintain that it subsequently died out until reintroduced by Thomas Becket (1118–70), who planted a fig tree at the Old Palace of the Archbishop of Canterbury at West Tarring in Sussex. The area was known for fig-growing and even now it has healthy productive trees. The earliest written reference to a British fig tree is in 1525, when Cardinal Pole is thought to have brought trees of the Marseilles type from Italy and planted them at Lambeth Palace. One grew to an enormous height but was destroyed in the severe winter of 1814. In 1648 a Doctor Pocock introduced a Syrian tree and planted it at Christ Church, Oxford. Despite a severe fire in 1803, it survived a further 30 years. Fig Sunday, as we have seen, is celebrated in Warwickshire with fig pudding on the fourth Sunday of Lent; in Buckinghamshire figs are eaten on Palm Sunday, possibly because our Lord blighted the barren fig tree after his entry into

Jerusalem; in the Lake District, on Good Friday, a drink made of ale, figs, sugar and ground ginger was the traditional brew; and in Cornwall there is a fig tree at St Newlyn East that is said to have come from the staff of St Newlina, a Christian martyr princess.

The figs that grew along the River Don in Sheffield are particularly interesting. They are recorded as having been about 70 years old in the 1920s when the steel industry was at its height. The explanation for their presence was that the water of the Don was used as a coolant by the steelworks, and therefore the river ran consistently at the right temperature for the germination of fig seeds from sewage outfalls. The Don is cooler now, and so there are no new trees, but some of the original ones have preservation orders on them.

Figs should be harvested in August and September. They keep in a cool place for several weeks. An airing-cupboard is an ideal place to dry them. Handle gently when turning them. The drying process should take no more than a week. Take care when picking figs in sunlight, as they may irritate sensitive skins. Do not allow the sap to come in contact with your eyes.

Towards meditation

Mark tells us that when Jesus blighted the fig tree he was hungry and had gone in search of fruit. He found only leaves, 'because it was not the season for figs'. The implication is almost that Jesus had made a mistake and was being unfair to the tree. It was in any case not a cultivated specimen and seems to have been growing on common land. Our Lord knew a great deal about the cultivation of figs and other essential food plants, as witness the parable in Luke already mentioned. Matthew reports Jesus' use of the blighting incident to teach his disciples about faith: 'If you have faith and never doubt, you will also be able to do such things, even to the moving of mountains.' But there are other interpretations from the rest of Christ's teaching, such as 'By their fruits shall ye know them' (Matt. 7:20). Leaves equal an outward profession of faith. Without the fruit Christ wants us to bear, we are useless. If our faith is not tended, if it is not active, we will be like the fruitless fig.

There was a practice known as 'caprification', which involved suspending the branches of a wild fig over a cultivated one, so that the fig wasp could do its work. In a similar way we need to be close to Christ, so that the fig wasp of the Spirit can bore into the wood of our souls and make us fruitful. Yet another interpretation, one that ties in with today's liturgy and particularly its gospel, is that the leafy but barren tree represents Jerusalem, where Jesus found much religious observance but little understanding, let alone welcome for him and his message. The blasting of the fig tree was an omen of the disaster that he prophesied would befall the city. In the gospel he is asked by the Jews who he is claiming to be. His truthful answer is taken by them as blasphemy, and as a sign of demonic possession. They do not recognize their true High Priest. Not only that, but they start picking up stones to throw at him. They are far from him, and like the fig are barren in their blindness and deafness. But Jesus 'hid himself and went out of the Temple'.

As we contemplate his second fall at the seventh Station of the Cross, may we be near to him, and may he not hide himself from us. At the third Station I thought of Christ falling to earth as a grain of wheat to bear a rich harvest, and now he falls on the way to bear the fruit of our salvation. But today I perceive also the awesome paradox and the appalling offence of our race, which he would forgive even as they crucified him, and forgives even as we crucify him now. The Lord of the Universe, our true High Priest, falls to the dust of his own creation under the weight of its sin. I wait in the silence and desolation of this moment. And then this year came the thought that the perfect Christ, who had no need to abase himself, is showing me what I must do when my overweening unjustified pride is hurt and my nose is rubbed into the dust of humiliation. It is such a small thing to offer, and yet I believe that, if every time it deservedly happens to me, I can fall with my Lord and not utter a word of complaint, if I can forgive and love those who inflict my small torments, then I am learning from him. I will be increasingly concerned with their welfare rather than with my own, and therein, sown by grace, lies the seed of my potential fruit.

Bible readings
Genesis 17:3–9: You shall be the father of the multitude of nations.
Psalm 105:4–9: God is mindful of his covenant.
Hebrews 4:14–15; 7:26–7; 9:11–12: Jesus the High Priest.
Matthew 21:18–22; Mark 11:12–14: The blasting of the barren fig tree.
John 8:51–9: Before Abraham was, I am.

Intercessions
For patience as gardeners; thanksgiving for the longevity of trees; for determination in the face of those who destroy them wantonly and

unnecessarily; thanksgiving for seasonal traditions that draw our attention to events in the life of Christ and to his message to us.

For an increase in faith, that we may bear fruit by being wholly grafted to Christ.

Place of spiritual retreat
With Jesus as he speaks to the Jews, in John 8.

FRIDAY WEEK FIVE IN LENT

CINQUEFOIL *Potentilla reptans*

Cultivation notes
This plant is regarded as a perennial lawn weed. It has five leaves and produces yellow flowers with orange stamens from June to August. In Culpeper's description, 'it creeps and spreads along the ground' with long slender strings, like the strawberry, to which it is related. The five leaves and five petals of cinquefoil, reminiscent of the wounds of Christ, explain its choice as today's plant. Exterminate it from your lawn if you must, and grow the dwarf shrubby *P. arbuscuta* for the same symbolism. It is not spectacular, but different varieties produce either white, yellow, tangerine or red flowers for almost six months of the year from early summer to autumn. They are deciduous and hardy. Prune in spring, cutting back young growth by a third.

History and lore
The name *potentilla* comes from the Latin *potens* and refers to the curative power of the plant. The leaves contain tannin, and this has been traditionally extracted to treat sore throats, mouth ulcers, cuts, sores, burns, sunburn, frostbite and even shingles. Roots are lifted in spring and dried for use in infusions.

Towards meditation
Sometimes cinquefoil produces seven leaves, and if by chance I find one of these, I may meditate on the seven last words of Christ from the cross, or on the seven sorrows rosary. However, it is more usual that today will remind me of the prophets. Its liturgy is permeated with Isaiah's prophecy of the passion and death of Jesus, and their redemptive purpose, and will

lead me to a re-reading of the relevant chapters. If one's faith needs bolstering, or one wants to renew and deepen it, or even if one merely wants to appreciate sheer poetry in the Spirit's furtherance of that faith, Isaiah, in my experience, fills the bill at any time but particularly on this fifth Friday in Lent. Meanwhile, in the gospel at Mass, the atmosphere of menace and danger to our Lord continues to build. The Jews want to stone him for allegedly blaspheming in his claim to be the Son of God. They want to arrest him, but he eludes them. His time, as we have already noted, is in his own hands, and has not yet come. But we know it is only a matter of days before Isaiah's prophecy will be fulfilled. For the present, however, Jesus crosses to the far side of the Jordan, where in the final hours many will come to believe.

At the eighth Station of the Cross, the women of Jerusalem who are following Jesus and 'lamenting' him may not have been among those believers; they may have been professional mourners. But to them is given Christ's penultimate prophecy, in which he tells them not to weep for him but for the fate of their city, which will be overthrown and ruined by the Romans within a few decades after his death. It will be so terrible that people will pray for the mountains to fall on them and bury them. The sacrifice of Christ on the cross was God's will and no amount of weeping on the road to Calvary could alter that fact. He would be raised to glory on the right hand of the Father; they would remain to endure the coming persecutions of their race, and we too weep bitterly for these. But I do not believe he was telling us not to grieve as we follow the Way of the Cross: rather that our grief must not be a 'professional' going through external motions that do not come from the depths of the heart and soul. Nor can I believe that Kathleen Ferrier was not feeling that deep grief when she recorded the Messiah aria 'He was despised'. The way she sings the word 'grief' itself convinces me of it. I always listen to her in the evening of this fifth Friday of Lent.

Bible readings
Isaiah 52: He shall be exalted and lifted up.
Isaiah 5: A man of sorrows, and acquainted with grief; surely he has borne our griefs and carried our sorrows, and with his stripes we are healed.
Colossians 1:21–2: The doers of evil, he has reconciled by his death.
1 Peter 2:21–4: He bore our sins in his body on the tree.
John 10:31–42: He escaped from their hands.

Intercessions

For sufferers from conditions traditionally treated by cinquefoil.

Thanksgiving for the prophets and for faith.

For the grace of true sorrow, and the courage to face and endure the future with our Lord.

Place of spiritual retreat

On the far side of the Jordan with the many who believed, as in John 10.

SATURDAY WEEK FIVE IN LENT

COLTSFOOT *Tussilago farfara*; *'Pas de l'âne'* (donkey's footstep); *'Filius ante patrem'* ('Son afore the Father')

Cultivation notes

This hardy perennial grows to a height of about 12 inches and is normally thought of as a weed. Its dandelion-yellow flowers can appear as early as February, but they remain closed in dull weather. In *The Folklore of Herbs*, Katherine Oldmeadow describes it as 'gold lighting up the drear winter's end'. The plant has heart-shaped leaves that arrive after the flowers and grow direct from the ground. These are covered with woolly down and are borne on clumps of thick, scaly, purplish stems. Coltsfoot likes sun and partial shade in a moist soil. The roots spread vigorously underground, bringing up soil nutrients that are beneficial to other plants. Coltsfoot is adaptable and root-cuttings will take quickly whether planted in spring or autumn.

History and lore

Coltsfoot is found in Europe, western Asia and North Africa. It was introduced to the United States from Europe and is now widespread over the northeastern states, growing from Newfoundland to Minnesota and south to New Jersey. Its Greek name was *bechion*, meaning 'cough plant', and Dioscorides recommended it to relieve persistent coughs. According to Pliny, the roots were burned over cypress charcoal and the smoke swallowed rather than inhaled. *Tussis* is Latin for cough, from which comes the modern French verb *tousser*. The English and French country names come from the shape of the leaves, and *Filius ante patrem* has its origins in the plant's habit of flowering before producing leaves. Coltsfoot was once such a famous remedy that it became the symbol of French apothecaries who painted its image on the doorposts of their shops. Poor country housewives are supposed to have used the silky white seed to stuff pillows, which must have taken a lot of coltsfoot as well as a lot of time. Children may enjoy collecting the seed to stuff diminutive soft furnishing for their doll's houses, but do remind them to leave some for the goldfinches, who love to line their nests with it. The young buds and flowers, and later the leaves, are a tasty addition to salads, and both the leaves and flowers are rich in vitamin C. An interesting and nutritious sandwich can be made from them, mixed with honey if sweetness is required. To treat bronchial complaints and stomach disorders make an infusion of dried leaves and flower heads, allow one teaspoon per cup of water, stand for five minutes, and then take two or three times a day. Boiled in milk, the leaves are a traditional remedy for coughs and colds. Add liquorice and honey to the infusion, or powder the leaves and smoke them. The flowers can be used to make wine, and the plant produces a yellowish-green dye. Cut flowers when they are open and the leaves when fully grown.

Towards meditation

Coltsfoot may seem a premature choice today as the entry of Christ into Jerusalem is not celebrated until tomorrow. However, apart from the Procession of Palms that takes place then, the Mass itself includes the reading of the passion from one of the synoptic Gospels, depending on the liturgical cycle. In other words, the joy of the preliminary procession is shortlived. Indeed, I suspect that the Church wants to move us on swiftly from the brief ecstatic welcome given to Jesus, which will prove an irony in coming days. The post-Vatican II missal marks tomorrow as Passion Sunday, with Palm Sunday below it in brackets. In spite of this, the day is still almost universally referred to as Palm Sunday. That is all very well, as long as we realize where the Church lays the emphasis. I have always thought that the Passion is read on the final Sunday of Lent to ensure its being heard by those who will not attend church on Good Friday, which (oddly to my mind) is not a holy day of obligation. And so because the passion will be my major concern tomorrow, I usually think today about that she-ass and her colt, and the way the Lord put them to his purpose. The incident, as Matthew tells us, is a fulfilment of Zechariah's prophecy (9:9b). But what if the disciples sent to untie the colt had been disobedient and refused to 'steal' it? What if the owners had scoffed at their reason,

'The Lord has need of it', and chased them off? What if the colt itself, which was unbroken, had refused to budge, as can be the way of its kind? But all goes smoothly, inexorably, because it is God's will.

The ass is thought of as a humble, rather low-class animal, inferior to the horse, and yet is loveable to us. He was present at the manger, and most probably carried our Lord to Egypt and back. Now he carries him towards the Cross, and I for one am prepared to believe the legend that the donkey bears its sign on his back for that reason. As G. K. Chesterton puts it:

> The tattered outlaw of the earth,
> Of ancient crooked will;
> Starve, scourge, deride me: I am dumb,
> I keep my secret still.
>
> Fools! For I also had my hour;
> One far fierce hour and sweet;
> There was a shout about my ears,
> And palms before my feet.[22]

It is a strange and paradoxical scene: the crowd is wild and abandoned in what could be seen as mass hysteria. This was the last thing wanted by the Jewish authorities in their delicate relationship with the Roman occupiers. It was most inconvenient and unsuitable at this point in time for anyone to claim to be the Messiah. But Jesus knew what he was doing and where he was headed, knew the lesson he was teaching. He, the Lord of the Universe, the great High Priest on whom the liturgy has been concentrating in recent days and again today, rides into Jerusalem on a humble donkey, overturning all usual notions of what it means to be royal and exalted. The kingship and high priesthood of Christ are of an altogether different nature. The gospel takes us forward. In it we have the verdict of Caiaphas, who probably did not understand the significance of his own words: 'It is expedient that one man should die for the people, and that the whole nation should not perish.' Almost certainly Caiaphas' statement was intended politically, but John leaves us in no doubt: Jesus would die, not for the nation only but to gather into one the children of God who are scattered abroad. We are those children, but we are not scattered when we celebrate our Lord's entry into the Holy City. We are there with him, among all the tribes who cry 'Hosanna'. But what is most wonderful is that we go forward to share the pasch with him, as St Gregory of Nazianzen says in today's second Office reading. And at the ninth Station of the Cross, we have the grave privilege of being close to him as he falls a third time, for the sake of Jew and Gentile alike.

Bible readings
Zechariah 9:9b: Behold your king comes to you riding on an ass.
Ezekiel 37:21–8: I will make them one nation.
Hebrews 8:1–13: The priesthood of Christ in the New Covenant.
Matthew 21:1–11: An ass and a colt with her.
Mark 11:1–10: An unbroken colt, on which no one had ever sat.
John 11:45–57: He should die not only for the nation.

Intercessions
For pharmacists.

Thanksgiving for the work of G. K. Chesterton and for all writers who stimulate our devotion to the truths of faith; thanksgiving for animals who speak to us of those truths through tradition and legend; thanksgiving for our destiny as the children Our Lord gathers together.

Place of spiritual retreat
Among the crowd as Christ enters Jerusalem, as in Matthew 21.

HOLY WEEK

PASSION SUNDAY (PALM SUNDAY)

PALM *Phoenix dactylifera*
DWARF FAN PALM *Chamaerops humilis*
DWARF NARCISSUS 'ANGELS' TEARS' *Narcissus triandrus albus*

Cultivation notes

The date palm is cultivated only in drier subtropical regions, but its wild relatives grow in the Canary Isles and eastward to India. These are available to us as houseplants, two popular varieties being *C. canariensis* (six feet) and *C. roebelenil* (three feet). The favourite palm court kentia palm, *Howea forsteriana* (eight feet), and the parlour palm, *Neanthe bella* (two feet), both make attractive alternatives. One of the most important things about palms is that there is only one growing point at the tip of each stem, so if the stem is cut back it will die. Kentia and parlour palms like a warmth of not less than 50°F and a winter night temperature of not more than 60°F. They can thrive in low light. Keep the soil slightly moist in winter, and water more generously in spring and summer. In a heated room, mist and sponge mature leaves occasionally and avoid draughts. Only repot if completely pot-bound and keep the soil compacted round the roots.

In the garden the dwarf fan palm is a misnomer because it can grow to a height of at least 15 feet. It is the only one native to Europe and grows wild on the Mediterranean coast. It was introduced to Britain in 1731 and was grown particularly in southwest England, where Torquay was able to advertise itself as the 'English Riviera' because of its palm trees. There is one at the end of our London street that has amazingly survived the winters of about 20 years. The fan palm also grows on the west coast of Scotland, warmed by the Gulf Stream. The evergreen fans of leaves are very susceptible to wind damage, so provide a sheltered site.

'Angels' tears' narcissus is a true dwarf, growing to a maximum height of eight inches. It will produce small, nodding, white or yellow flowers in Lent and, if it is to be an early Easter, on Palm Sunday too.

History and lore

In early Old Testament times the fruit of the palm was so poor that the Talmud excluded it from the tithe law of first fruits, but by the time of the Psalmist it had come to typify grace, elegance and uprightness: 'The righteous flourish like the palm tree' (Ps. 92:12). By 165 BC it had acquired significance in the restoration of the Temple, which the Jews entered 'with praise and palm branches' (1 Macc. 13:51); 'bearing ... fronds of palm, they offered hymns and thanksgiving' (2 Macc. 10:7). For contemporaries of Our Lord the palm was firmly established as a symbol of victory and rejoicing. John must have been certain that his first readers would recognize their significance: 'Behold a great multitude ... standing before the throne and before the Lamb, clothed in white robes, with palm branches in their hands' (Rev. 7:9). It is hardly surprising therefore that in Christian art the palm came to represent spiritual victory and the triumph of divine love. Medieval pilgrims were known as 'palmers' because they carried the palm for its spiritual significance. Shakespeare knew this, and when in *Romeo and Juliet* the lovers meet for the first time (Act I, scene v), he gives them a sonnet to share, full of the imagery of pilgrimhood, punning on the palms of their hands that meet in an attitude of prayer, and on the palms of pilgrims. Thus he elevates their love as above the common, demonstrates the perfect unity of their sharing, and symbolizes the sacrament of their impending marriage: 'For saints have hands that pilgrims' hands do touch, / And palm to palm is holy palmers' kiss.'

History of Palm Sunday ritual

The blessing and procession of palms is thought to date from the fifth century, and it was definitely in place by the time of the Venerable Bede (d. 735). Historians have conjectured that palms were used in the medieval Mystery plays and that as a result the Church began to bless them, thus turning mere stage props into sacramentals. The branches would probably not have been of true palm at that stage, and it was the old English custom to use our native willow or yew instead. In parts of Kent the yew is still called a palm, whilst throughout rural Ireland the churchyard yew was always used on Palm Sunday and referred to as the palm. At Wells Cathedral there is a quiet little graveyard known as 'Palm Churchyard', and in the middle of it is an ancient yew. In *Lore and Legend of the English Church*,[23] G. S. Tyack notes London churchwardens' accounts that allude to the purchase of willow and box for Palm Sunday. In South Wales and Shropshire the day was also known as Flowering Sunday, when graves were adorned with fresh flowers, and an old Gloucestershire belief was that seed sown on Palm Sunday would bear double flowers. As the centuries unrolled, the palms ceremony before high Mass became longer and longer and more and more complicated. The reforms of Vatican II cut away a great deal, but the ritual thankfully retains the central motif of homage to Christ triumphant and heightens and intensifies it. Nowadays palms are distributed at the altar-rail, at the door of the church, or at a prearranged local open-air meeting-place. The latter is the practice of my own church, and I approve it because it allows public testimony of our gratitude and homage to Christ the King, who entered death for the sake of us all. Palms blessed and gospel read, we sing as we walk back to church.

Another open-air assembly I love takes place at the Cistercian nunnery at Echourgnac in the Dordogne. The faithful arrive early with branches from their gardens or local hedgerows and wait outside the abbey church in an atmosphere of subdued excitement. At last the nuns come out of the enclosure with their chaplain, all bearing branches cut from within their *domaine*. The branches are blessed, and after the gospel the community leads us, singing, into church.

Whatever the local variation in ritual, it is still the universal practice to burn undistributed palms. Their ashes are kept until the following year to be used at the ceremony of Ash Wednesday, when the whole Lenten cycle begins again. It would be unbearably and unutterably depressing if we did not, through Christ, have certain hope of winning the palm of eternal victory.

Towards meditation

The palm as well as the laurel was given by the Greeks and Romans to victors in their games, so any Roman who witnessed the entry of Christ into Jerusalem must have been interested to see that it had the same significance in Jewish culture as it had in his own. He could not know, and indeed neither could the majority of the wildly rejoicing crowd, that Christ's victory was to be not in some game but over death itself. They could not know that he would rise from the dead, and that the palms thrown in his path would come to signify immortality, especially for the martyrs, who through Christ would also conquer death.

As I intimated yesterday, the modern Palm Sunday liturgy is particular in its sharp juxtaposition of joy and sorrow, pulling us within the space of an hour or so through the whole gamut of emotional and spiritual response to

Christ. I go home with the words 'They laid Jesus there' (John 19:40b) ringing in my head. They had to leave the body of the Lord, not knowing, not daring to believe that he would rise. What desolation, what confusion, what fear and sorrow they must have experienced. It is very different for us, and we should thank God that as the sun sets on Palm Sunday we know truths unknown to the wild Jerusalem throng and unknown at the time to those who buried Jesus later that week. And it is these truths that cause our joy and sorrow today. If the palm stands for our joy, then the little 'Angels' tears' narcissus, so named, I guess, because of its drooping flower-heads, stands for our sorrow.

At home I go back to the Stations of the Cross, to be confronted with Christ being stripped of his garments before crucifixion, and want to cry out: 'How could they have been so coarse, so arrogant, so vulgar, insensitive and irreverent?' And then I remember the occasions when I have been all of these things, when I have been overly concerned with my own appearance, when I have failed to be aware of the sensitivities of others. Then I remember that every time I have failed in those ways, I have stripped Christ just as much as those I now have the temerity to criticize. And yet he forgives me as he forgave them. And I am back to amazed joy. Palm Sunday: a day of paradox indeed.

Bible readings
Zechariah 9:9: Rejoice Jerusalem, your king is coming to you.
Isaiah 50:4–7: I set my face like flint.
Acts 13:26–30a: They did not know.
Hebrews 16:1–18: We are made holy through the offerings of Christ.
1 Peter 4:13–14: Have some share in the sufferings of Christ.
1 Peter 5:10–11: He will confirm, strengthen and support you.
Philippians 2:6–11: But God raised him high.
Matthew 21·1–11; Mark 11:1–10; Luke 19:28–40: The commissioning of the colt.
Luke 22:14–56: Are you the King of the Jews? Thou sayest it.

Intercessions
For donkeys and those who run sanctuaries for them; for those who grow and prepare palms for distribution in churches on Palm Sunday; for sacristans, vergers, readers, servers, parish administrators and church-wardens as they approach one of the busiest and most demanding times of their year.

Thanksgiving for the Mystery plays; for teachers; thanksgiving for the liturgy and for plants that help us to celebrate it.

For grace to celebrate today with increased understanding, and with the right balance between joy and sorrow.

Place of spiritual retreat
Among the crowd as Jesus rides into Jerusalem, as in Matthew 21, Mark 11, Luke 19 or John 12.

MONDAY IN HOLY WEEK

SPIKENARD *Nardostachys grandiflora*; nard

Cultivation notes
Spikenard is a dwarf perennial shrub that reaches a height of up to 12 inches. Both stem and fibrous roots are highly aromatic, and the small purple-pink flowers appear in late summer. Propagate by sowing ripe seed. The plant does not like rich soil and prefers a cool, gritty and moist root-run. Give it a position in partial shade, where it will be protected from midday sun. Popular as a rock-garden plant in Victorian times, it is not much seen nowadays, although there are specimens at Kew Gardens. The plant is related to valerian and is thought to be medicinally superior to it.

History and lore
Spikenard is native to the rocky ledges and open scrubby slopes of the Himalayas and is found from Uttar Pradesh to China. The name comes from the Greek *nardos*, 'nard', and *stachys*, meaning 'ear' or 'spike'. Oil of spikenard is obtained from the roots, which are dried and then used to make perfume and cosmetics. Rejuvenating properties have been claimed for it, and it allegedly improves digestion, calms nerves and lowers blood pressure. The herb is astringent as well as aromatic, and in modern herbalism decoctions are made for the internal treatment of insomnia,

depression and tension. These can also be applied externally as a deodorant or to soothe rashes. The perfume was a highly valuable commodity in the Roman Empire, and according to Judas Iscariot (John 12:5) was worth 300 denarii per pound. The fact that the average daily wage of the labourer was a single denarius brings home to us what a luxury it really was. According to F. Nigel Hepper,[24] the nard mentioned in the Song of Solomon was obtained from camel grass (*Cymbopogon schoenanthus*). This grew in the Arabian and North African deserts and was used throughout classical times (*nerd* in Hebrew, *lardu* in Assyrian). However, the nard of Solomon does prefigure the pure and precious nard used to anoint Jesus in Mark 14 and John 12: 'While the king was on his couch, my nard gave forth its fragrance' (Song 1:12). By the time of Jesus this 'real nard' was exported from its native land in sealed alabaster boxes – no wonder it was expensive. The seal would be broken and the perfume released only if a specially honoured guest in the house was to be anointed.

Towards meditation

Today's gospel is John's account of the anointing of Jesus by Mary of Bethany. According to him, a supper was made for Jesus there. He does not say where in Bethany it took place but that Martha served and Lazarus was among those at table with the Lord. Mark tells us that the supper was at the house of Simon the Leper, and although he knows this detail he does not seem to know the identity of the woman who anointed Christ and does not mention the Bethany sisters and their brother in relation to the event. We know that John was one of a select band of three who went almost everywhere with Jesus, and to my humble mind this has the flavour of an eyewitness account. He is also prepared to hazard a lot more about the motive of Judas Iscariot when he complained about extravagance and suggested the ointment should have been sold and the money given to the poor. John is acerbic and openly accusatory: 'Not that he cared for the poor but because he was a thief, and as he had the money-box he used to take what was put into it' (John 12:6). If Mark knows this, he keeps his counsel and merely says, 'there were some' who objected, before reporting Jesus' rebuke, which in John is clearly directed at Judas. But Mark does add a wonderful detail of commendation to Jesus' defence of Mary's action: 'And truly I say to you, wherever the gospel is preached in the whole world, what she has done will be told in memory of her.'

Another difference between the two accounts is that John says Mary 'anointed the feet of Jesus, and wiped his feet with her hair', whereas Mark says she broke the flask and poured it over his head. I hope they are both a true record, because then the symbolism becomes even more rich. Jesus himself refers to the connection of nard with anointing for burial: 'she has anointed my body beforehand for burying' (Mark) and 'let her keep it for the day of my burial' (John). In John, Mary's anointing of Our Lord's feet is an act of profound obeisance, homage and an intimately spiritual love for her Master, showing that she welcomed him as the most honoured guest ever received, and perhaps even sorrow for the events that she guessed might soon take place. If she anointed Christ's head as in Mark then he is shown to us as King and High Priest. It is possible that Mary knew all of these significances. And whether or not she foresaw the death of Jesus, she would certainly have been anxious for him. All his followers knew the danger, and Mary would have known what pressure her Lord's tireless ministry of preaching and healing placed on him. Jesus would have been physically and mentally refreshed by Mary's anointing. He would also have recognized the spontaneity of pure love. And so he says: 'Let her alone, why do you trouble her? She has done a beautiful thing to me' (Mark 14:6). True enough, the poor are always with us and we must care for them in him, and him in them. But when he comes as our personal guest, as he always does when invited, even though we may not be conscious of his presence, our reaction should imitate Mary's. Our business is to honour, love and care for him in just her way, and in the coming week to dine at *his* table, to stay with him throughout his passion, to face the awful fact of the crucifixion, presented to us in the eleventh Station, and to acknowledge that our sins are the nails that held him to the Cross. So we must stay at its foot until he is taken down and buried, praying that he may say of us, 'Let them alone; why do you trouble them? They have done a beautiful thing to me.'

Bible readings
Hebrews 10:35–6: Do not throw away your confidence, which has a great reward.
Luke 21:19: By your endurance you will gain your lives.
Jeremiah 18:20b: Remember how I stood before thee to turn away thy wrath.
Jeremiah 31:2: The people who survived the sword found grace in the wilderness.
Isaiah 42:1-7: Behold my chosen, in whom my soul delights.

Mark 14:3–11: A woman came with an alabaster flask of pure nard.
John 11:1–9: Mary took a pound of costly ointment of pure nard.

Intercessions
For gardeners, particularly at Kew; for the peoples of India, China, Nepal and Tibet; for sufferers from high blood pressure, insomnia, depression and nervous tension.

That we may demonstrate our love for Jesus in an extravagance acceptable to him; that we may love him and endure with him this week and always.

Place of spiritual retreat
With Jesus and Mary at Bethany, as in John 11 and Mark 14.

TUESDAY IN HOLY WEEK

JUDAS TREE *Cercis siliquastrum*

Cultivation notes
The Judas tree is native to the Mediterranean region and in Britain is capable of reaching a height of 20 feet. Mine, in France – a mere 5-foot shrub when we bought the house in 1989 – is now about 25 feet tall. Each April clusters of three to six rosy, purple flowers appear direct from the naked branches, their form witnessing to the tree's membership of the pea family. Heart-shaped leaves appear after flowering. The Judas tree is susceptible to northern winds and grows best on a south-facing wall in dry, chalky soil. Mine is east facing, but benefits from full sun until early afternoon. Green pods ripen to purple in autumn, so there are very few months of the year when the Judas tree lacks ornamental interest.

History and lore

The common English name is thought to come from a Greek tradition that Judas Iscariot hanged himself from a *Cercis*, and its crooked branches are said to be the result of his dead weight. The flowers are perceived to ooze like drops of blood from the branches; other ideas are that they represent Christ's tears at Judas' treachery, or that their colour is that of the traitor's blush of shame. The real reason for the name is probably more prosaic, and it is possibly a corruption of Judaea tree, from the area in the Holy Land where it is common.

Towards meditation

The gospel today is John's account of Christ's prediction as to who will betray him. I find it salutary to have a Judas tree, not by my own design or choice; it is lovely, but I never pass it without a shiver in my soul. Its loveliness shows what we all have the potential to be, but on the other hand its association with the one who betrayed Jesus is a sharp reminder that we all also have the potential for evil. Even though he was in daily contact with the supreme virtue of the Lord of Life, Judas chose sin and death: 'The Son of Man goes as it is written of him, but woe to that man by whom the Son of Man is betrayed! It would have been better for that man if he had not been born.'

Many of today's liturgical texts deal with the way in which God's actions and designs reverse human notions of wisdom and folly. The Cross itself is a supreme example. Even on a human level, in a group of twelve men, there will be at least one more likely than the others to exercise his free will in favour of letting 'Satan enter into him'. None of the disciples started out as saints. I think they were chosen as representative of ordinary men, and it would have been surprising had there not been a Judas among them. And many of them had faults: James and John argued about who was to be the greatest in the Kingdom; Peter overestimated his own loyalty and courage before Jesus' arrest; they all ran away from the Garden of Gethsemane after Christ's arrest; and after his resurrection Thomas doubted. Surely there can be no sainthood without acknowledgement of our weakness, none without doubts that are borne and overcome, none without total love for and trust in God, and none without resisting evil and its temptations. Satan will not give up until after the final battle. Whether one believes those words literally or metaphorically, we have to recognize that the 'devil' is a force that denies and fights the glory, love, beauty and goodness of the Supreme God. Symbolically or actually cast out of heaven because of his rebellion, he and his cohorts were quelled by St Michael. God then had Lucifer to deal with; Christ had him making use of the personality of Judas. But there is a difference. Judas repented and returned the 30 pieces of silver. At the end he acknowledged his sin against the innocent Jesus. But where then could he turn? No wonder he despaired. Perhaps that is what Christ meant by saying that it would have been better for Judas not to have been born than to know the despair that led to suicide. Hell may not be Dante's *Inferno*, but it must be the state of having glimpsed God and yet knowing eternally that he cannot be approached nor seen again.

Making a decision about the eternal destiny of Judas is not really our business though, and we do better to turn to the second Office reading, where St Basil, in his *Book on the Holy Spirit,* has dug the gold nugget out of today's liturgical mine – that there is one death for the world and one resurrection from the dead, and that this is through the sufferings, Cross, burial and resurrection of Jesus Christ our Lord. I take the reading with me when I go to the twelfth Station: Jesus dies on the Cross.

Bible readings
Zechariah 12:10–11a: I will pour out a spirit of kindness and prayer.
Hebrews 12:1–13: With Christ we go forward to the struggle.
Philippians 2:8: Humility and obedience.
1 Corinthians 1:18–19: The Cross is folly to those on the way to ruin.
1 Corinthians 1:22–30: Christ nailed to the Cross is the power and wisdom of God.
John 13:21–38: Christ predicts his betrayal by Judas; Peter's denial.

Intercessions
For those tempted to despair; for the grace to be like Peter and weep bitterly over our weakness, and like John to follow Christ to the Cross.

That in the light of the Spirit our eyes may be opened to the things we need to see and understand.

Place of spiritual retreat
At the Last Supper, as in John 13.

WEDNESDAY IN HOLY WEEK

ELDER *Sambucus nigra*

Cultivation notes

The common elder is deciduous and may be kept as a shrub or allowed to grow up to 30 feet. Masses of creamy-white flowers appear in late spring, followed by the familiar black berries in late summer. It is not grown in gardens as extensively as it once was and has been superseded by ornamental varieties. Of these the hardy *S. nigra* 'Aurea' is popular for its golden leaves and ability to withstand extremes of frost and sun. It grows to a height of about 20 feet if left to its own devices. *S. nigra* 'Guinero Purple' has purple-bronze leaves and can also reach 20 feet; its flowers are pale pink. Wild elder grows in profusion where the nitrogen content in the soil is high, for instance, near abandoned dwellings, in old churchyards and near rabbit warrens. Mine, on the site of an old hen-house, was, like the Judas tree, a mere shrub 14 years ago, but has now attained its full height. Ornamental varieties like rich, moist soil in sun or partial shade. Propagate by softwood cuttings in summer and by hardwood cuttings in winter. Do not prune hard if flowers and fruit are required.

History and lore

The elder is found in Europe, Asia, North Africa and the United States, and has been cultivated for centuries. *Nigra* is Latin for black and refers to the dark colour of the bark; *sambucus* is from the Greek *sambuke* for musical pipe. As generations of children have found to their pleasure, the hollowed-out stems can be used to make whistles and pea-shooters. This is reflected in the word 'elder', which comes from Anglo-Saxon *ellaern* relating to hollowness. In English lore the tree symbolizes zeal. This is surprising since historically it has had a very mixed significance. Many superstitions endow it with evil properties, while others invest it with the power to repel malign forces. The former may have originated from the old legend that elder, and not yesterday's *Cercis*, was the tree from which Judas hanged himself. (This is confusing as in some parts of Britain the elder may still be referred to as the Judas tree.) The belief dates back at least to the fourteenth century. As William Langland (c. 1330–c. 1386) wrote in *Piers Plowman*:[25]

> Judas he gaped
> With Jewen silver
> And sithen on an elder
> Hanged himselve.

There is also a reference (c. 1357) in Sir John Mandeville's book of his travels: 'Fast by is the elder tree on which Judas hanged himself', and Shakespeare alludes to the tradition in *Love's Labour's Lost* (Act V, scene ii, line 607). The jelly-like fungus that sometimes attacks elder bark is called Jew's or Judas' ear. Elder was not used for shipbuilding or furniture-making as it was believed the wood warped, cracked and broke. Other superstitions were that it was risky to make a cradle from it, in case the tree spirit Mother Elder might emerge and attack the child; and it should never be used as domestic fuel as it may raise the devil or bring a death to the family. (In fact it doesn't burn well, being very smoky.) Converse beliefs were that it repelled witches; that anyone who planted the tree near his dwelling would be safe from all danger, and particularly from lightning. For this reason it was often planted near stables or nailed over doorways in the shape of a cross. Branches were buried with the dead or planted near graves, and hearse-drivers carried a whip of elder, all with the purpose of protecting the soul of the deceased from evil. These customs probably had their origins in the belief that Our Lord's Cross was made of elder-wood, which in its turn may have sprung from the fourth verse of the hymn *Vexilla Regis* by Venantius Fortunatus (530–609). The purple mentioned might have been taken as a reference to the colour of elderberries, as well as to the divine royalty that graced the tree of the Cross:

> Most royally empurpled o'er
> How beauteous thy stem doth shine
> How glorious was its lot to touch
> Those limbs so holy and divine.

Elder was believed to cure a tremendous range of ailments, including toothache, melancholy, dog-bites and warts. All parts of the plant have either a culinary or horticultural or household use. Elder-wood is hard and yellowish white and has traditionally been used to make small wooden items such as toys, combs and spoons. Its reputation as the medicine chest of country people is well founded. The berries have particular curative properties and are rich in vitamin C, while the flowers contain an anti-inflammatory acid. Both fruit and flowers have diuretic, anti-catarrhal effects, soothe irritation and can be used to treat influenza, sinusitis and fever. The juice of the berries is good for rheumatism; the leaves and bark are effective in the treatment of minor burns and chilblains; and the flowers are soothing to sore eyes, inflamed skin and mouth ulcers. An elder planted near the compost heap will hasten the rotting process, and bruised branches will repel aphids from fruit trees. The leaves, boiled and strained, make a 'green' insecticide, and when rubbed fresh onto the skin they are an effective insect repellent for at least half an hour. Elderflowers give a raisin-like flavour to stewed fruit, jellies, sauces, ketchups and preserves. They make a delicious 'champagne', while the berries produce an acceptable, healthy red wine. (If space allows, it is worth having two trees so that you can make both wines in the same year.) 'Elderberry Rob', a thick syrup made from the berries, is probably the most versatile product of the tree. In various strengths it can be used as cough medicine or a soothing nightcap. Diluted with ice, soda water and a dash of lemon it makes a refreshing summer drink; poured cold over hot rice pudding it ennobles the end of an English kitchen lunch; and, served cold with home-made vanilla ice-cream, it elevates the latter to dinner-party worthiness.

Pick flowers when fully open in late spring, dry whole, and then strip from the stalks with a fork. Harvest berries in late summer and use fresh; strip the bark in autumn while leaves are still green, or in late winter before new buds appear.

To make Elderberry Rob: Wash five cups of fresh elderberries and strip from their stalks. Place in a saucepan with five tablespoons of water, cover and simmer gently over a low heat, occasionally crushing the berries with a wooden spoon. Strain through a sieve, pressing the berries with the back of the spoon to extract all the juice. Return juice to pan adding a pound of sugar for each pint of juice. Bring slowly to the boil, stirring continuously until the sugar has dissolved, then boil for five to ten minutes in the uncovered pan, until the Rob is thick and syrupy. Remove from heat and skim. Cool and pour into clean bottles and cork, or use screw-top jars.

Towards meditation
The elder is suitable today because of its traditional connections with Judas and the Cross of Christ. The gospel includes Matthew's description

of Judas' treacherous transaction with the chief priests. Having been paid
the infamous 30 pieces of silver, he goes away looking for an opportunity
to betray Jesus. (It is for this reason that in parts of northern England the
Wednesday of Holy Week is still known as 'Spy Wednesday'.) For the
second day running our attention is drawn to the perfidy of Judas, who
barefacedly asks the Lord, when all at the table are questioning the
identity of the prophesied traitor, 'Is it I, Master?' Today's liturgy is
rooted in Old Testament prophecy applied to Christ's passion, and there
is writing from Paul that comments on its nature, purpose and result. But
for now the shadow of the Cross is beginning to block out the light. Until
the Easter vigil its painful, dark and shameful aspects are all we can see.
Any tree may inspire us to meditate on these. As Joseph Mary Plunkett
(1887–1915) wrote: 'His crown of thorns is twined with every thorn; / His
cross is every tree.'[26] But standing under my elder this year, I remembered
'Woefully Arrayed', by an unknown medieval English poet. The poem is
extremely moving in its directness and lack of artifice or ornament; it most
forcibly conveys Christ's love for us and his desire that we should love him:

> Thus naked am I nailed, O man, for thy sake.
> I love thee, then love me. Why sleepest thou? Awake!
> Remember my tender heart-root for thee brake
> . . .
> Dear brother, none other thing I desire
> But give me thy heart free, to reward mine hire.
> I am he that made the earth, water and fire.
> . . .
> I have purveyed a place full clear
> For mankind, whom I have bought dear.[27]

Now seems the right moment to turn to the thirteenth Station: Jesus is
taken down from the Cross. Those of us who have watched the agony of a
dying loved one will know a little of the terrible mixture of relief, sorrow
and desolation that must have been the lot of those who ministered to Our
Lord at this point, and they will know something of the love and
gentleness with which they carried out their service.

Leaving the elder, I remembered the solemn and remarkable services
of Tenebrae that were the Matins and Lauds of the Wednesday, Thursday
and Friday of Holy Week and used to be celebrated on the evenings of
those days. The lessons were from the Lamentations of Jeremiah, and
during the Offices the candles in the sanctuary were extinguished one by

one, the last one being placed behind the altar during the singing of *'Christus factus est'* (Christ was obedient even unto death), thus symbolizing the darkness that fell upon the earth at the moment of his death. After prayers the clergy would make a noise with their books as a reminder of the earthquake that accompanied the darkness. At the end, the sole candle was brought out and relit as an emblem of the Risen Saviour. The modern Office texts are different, and if the public service of Tenebrae takes place at all it will be in a cathedral and even then in the morning, which to my mind defeats the whole idea. And so in the absence of Tenebrae in church, this evening I begin reading the Lamentations of Jeremiah, the five short chapters to be completed before bedtime on Good Friday. The verses from Jeremiah used to be sung to a tune that has been described as the saddest melody in the whole of music. Certainly, to my ear, it is one of the most beautiful chants in the Church's repertoire. I listened to it this year on disc,[28] and as always it seemed perfectly to convey the sorrow Jeremiah felt at the desolation of Jerusalem, and therefore *our* grief over the sufferings and death of Jesus.

Bible readings

Psalm 41:9; John 13:18b: He who ate my bread has lifted his heel against me.

Isaiah 50:4–9: I gave my back to those who struck me.

Psalm 69: It is for thy sake that I have borne reproach.

Philippians 2:8–11: Christ became obedient unto death.

Hebrews 9:28: Christ was offered once to bear the sins of many.

Ephesians 4:32–5:2: Walk in love, as Christ loved us.

Hebrews 12:14–29: You have come to the city of the living God, the heavenly Jerusalem.

Lamentations of Jeremiah 1:2: For these things I weep.

Matthew 26:14–25: From that moment he looked for an opportunity to betray him.

Intercessions

Thanksgiving for the writings of William Langland, William Shakespeare and Joseph Mary Plunkett; for the composers of plainchant and for the polyphony of the Renaissance.

For those tempted to follow evil ways, and for those who have succumbed.

For grace to resist the false attraction of evil and superstition; for time during this week to give Christ our wholehearted, undivided love and attention.

Place of spiritual retreat
At the Last Supper, as in Matthew 26.

THURSDAY IN HOLY WEEK (MAUNDY THURSDAY)

PASQUE FLOWER *Pulsatilla vulgaris*

Cultivation notes
This small, hardy, clump-forming perennial is related to the anemone. In April and May it produces nodding, bell-like violet flowers before its leaves. The stamens are golden and prominent, and the delicate silky stems grow to a height of about 12 inches. It appreciates a sunny position in well-drained soil and does not like being disturbed, so it is best to plant root-cuttings in winter or to sow seed under cover in summer. Pasque flower has sadly become rare in the wild because of lost habitat, although it can still be found among grasses on chalky soil. Two varieties are available for the garden: the white *P. vulgaris alba* and the red variety, *P. vulgaris rubra*.

History and lore
Various species of the genus are native to Eurasia and northern Africa. The common English name was given by the herbalist John Gerard (1545–1612) who explained: 'They floure for the most part about Easter, which has moved mee to name it Pasque-Floure or Easter floure.' Modern herbalism claims that elixirs and tinctures made from the flowering plant

are effective against headaches, neuralgia, insomnia, hyperactivity, septicaemia, whooping cough and skin infections. It can cause diarrhoea, vomiting and convulsions, and therefore internal consumption is best avoided. However, the flowers yield a green dye, traditionally used for painting Easter eggs.

Towards meditation
The three colours of pasque flower make it an ideal choice today: the violet represents Christ's royalty, his sorrow in the Garden of Gethsemane, our grief at his suffering and our repentance for the sins that crucified him; the ruby red speaks of the blood he shed for us and the wine he consecrated at the Last Supper; the white signifies the purity of his sacrifice on the Cross and in the Eucharist; while the bright golden stamens in the species and two varieties symbolize his high priesthood and kingship.

Liturgically, and therefore spiritually, Maundy Thursday is one of the richest days in the Church's year. In the morning she restocks her sacramentals cupboard with enough holy oils for the coming year. Work precludes most of us from being present, and the evening Mass of the Lord's Supper is the high-point of the day, with its joyful ringing of bells at the Gloria, after which they and the organ remain silent until the Easter Vigil. In this way the Church signals her entry into a period of deep gravity and solemnity. There is the stripping of the altars at the end, bringing us face to face with the stark prospect of tomorrow and possibly symbolizing the stripping of Christ before his crucifixion. Some of the most beautiful and ancient chant is used at this Mass, from the hauntingly lovely *Ubi caritas* to the magnificent *Pange lingua* of Thomas Aquinas.

I came from broad-church Anglicanism to Catholicism at the age of 16. Thoroughly grounded in scripture and the Book of Common Prayer, I knew *Hymns Ancient and Modern* like the back of my hand and loved Matins and Evensong and the chants of the psalms. I had been confirmed and took Holy Communion once a month. But something was missing. When I was confronted with the Catholic belief in the Real Presence of Christ, it hit me like a thunderbolt and was at the heart of my conversion. I dread to think of the life I would have led without it, and so for me Maundy Thursday is an occasion for profound thanksgiving and celebrated as the birthday of the core of my Catholic faith.

It is no accident that the Last Supper takes place at the Jewish festival of Passover. I love to hear Christ described as the Pasch because it takes us back to the Judaic roots of our religion and gives strength to our souls in that continuity. His life and death are prefigured throughout the Old Testament in Abel, Isaac, Jacob, Joseph, Moses and David and in the writings of psalmists and prophets. Mellitus of Sardis reflects on this in the second Office reading. 'But he who had no bone broken upon the cross, was not corrupted in the earth, for he rose from the dead and raised up man from the depths of the grave.' Christ is our Pasch not only because he invites us to partake of his body and blood at the Passover feast but also because mystically he is the Passover of our salvation.

The *mandatum*, the priest's ceremonial washing of the feet of members of the congregation, is the origin of the name 'Maundy' and draws attention to two of the day's central themes: service and love. *Mandatum* means a command, but the close *mundare* coincidentally means to cleanse. Both remind us of Christ's words: 'You ought to wash one another's feet.' The gospel underlines the lesson: 'Love one another as I have loved you; by this all men will know that you are my disciples.'

We know from Matthew and Mark that Jesus and his disciples sang a hymn before going out to the Mount of Olives, and so it is fitting that we sing a hymn as the Lord is carried to the altar of repose, our annual replication of the Garden of Gethsemane. Luke adds touchingly that Jesus went there as was his custom. At times of stress and crisis we too tend to flee to a calm and familiar place. Jesus the man was no different. But in the Garden of Gethsemane he would bear the greatest mental and spiritual stress and crisis ever known. And it was there that our salvation was made sure, with his prayer: 'Nevertheless, not my will but thine be done' (Luke 22:42b). I love Maundy Thursday because at its end the Church gives us the opportunity to answer Christ positively when he asks the question: 'Could you not watch with me one hour?' At times during the watch the flickering candles and heavy scent of flowers combine to hypnotic effect and I share and fight with the disciples the overwhelming desire to sleep, but I thank God that like them I am given the privilege of being there. In France, the shortage of priests results in our having one of the Triduum celebrations only once every few years in the village church. This year we had the Good Friday liturgy, so it could be as much as six years before we have the Mass of the Lord's Supper again. And so, in the lean years, I keep watch in my garden sanctuary. It is a strangely shattering and more demanding experience, probably because it is uncomfortably nearer to the reality of what happened than the safe, warm familiarity of church ambience and ritual. In any case, whether in church or garden, I have faith that Jesus knows my presence and I know his. Before leaving I think ahead awhile to the last Station: Jesus is laid in the tomb. And I reflect that tomorrow we must go back to the beginning, and share, God willing, more deeply in the events that we have, so to speak, rehearsed over the last fortnight through our daily reflections on the 14 Stations of the Way of the Cross.

Bible readings
Exodus 12:1–14: The Passover.
Lamentations of Jeremiah 3:4: I am the man who has seen affliction under the rod of his wrath.
Psalm 116:12–18: I will lift up the cup of salvation.
1 Corinthians 10:16: The cup is our participation in the blood of Christ; the bread, in his body.
Hebrews 4:14–5:10: In Jesus we have the supreme high priest.
Hebrews 9:1–12: He entered the Holy Place securing our redemption.
1 Corinthians 13:13: Faith, hope and love: the greatest is love.
John 13:1-15: The *mandatum*.
John 13:34–5: Love one another as I have loved you.
Matthew 26:36–46: My soul is sorrowful even unto death.
Mark 14:26–42: Not what I will, but what thou wilt.
Luke 22:39–46: Rise and pray that you may not enter into temptation.

Intercessions
For sufferers from ailments treated by the pasque flower.

Thanksgiving for writers who have drawn our attention to the religious symbolism of plants; thanksgiving for the liturgy of Maundy Thursday, that we may enter into it more deeply with each successive year; for the music of the liturgy, for the anonymous composers of ancient chant, and for the psalm chants of the Anglican Church; for the *Pange lingua* of Thomas Aquinas.

For grace to fulfil Christ's commandment to love and serve each other; for grace to stay awake in the Garden of Gethsemane.

Thanksgiving for the Eucharist.

Place of spiritual retreat
In the Garden of Gethsemane, as in Matthew 26, Mark 14, or Luke 22.

GOOD FRIDAY: THE CELEBRATION OF THE LORD'S PASSION

PASSION FLOWER

Passiflora caerulea

Cultivation notes

In the east and north of England this perennial flowering climber needs to be grown in a conservatory, but in warmer areas it can be tried against a southwest-facing wall, fence or trellis. Once established, it can reach a height of 20 feet, and the slightly fragrant flowers can be as much as three inches in diameter. These are produced from June to September and are followed by orange, plum-shaped fruits. Plant in May, in compost-enriched and, if possible, slightly acid soil, in a position where the plant will benefit from full sun. Train, and also layer the stems in April. I know of a *P. caerulea* that grows as a front garden hedge of a house amid the polluted environment of suburban London. A vigorous climber by nature, it probably flowered profusely from being cut back to hedge form. The books say that frost protection should be given during winter. None ever seems to be given to the London specimen. Worse, during last winter, the householder decided to replace the low brick wall in front of his passion flower. It was a relief to see that the workmen had obviously been instructed to disturb the roots as little as possible, with the result that the following June, although it did not flower, its bare branches were being trained against the new wall, and it had put forth green shoots. Hardier varieties than *P. caerulea* are *P.* 'Constance Eliot', with its large fragrant ivory flowers, and the pale violet American *P. incarnata*. If you do not have a garden, or you wish to be on the safe side, all these varieties can be grown indoors where space allows.

History and lore

P. caerulea came to Britain from South America about 1699. It was originally named *Flos passionis*, but Linnaeus changed this to *Passiflora*. It is mentioned in an old verse that names flowers connected with the Christian year: 'The Passion-floure long has blowed / To betoken us signs of the Holy Rood.' *P. incarnata* arrived in Britain in 1629, the year of Parkinson's *Paradisus*. He was scathing: 'Some superstitious Jesuits would faine make me believe that in this plant are to be seene all the markes of our Saviour's Passion.' He dismisses this as being 'true as the sea burnes'. One wonders whether he had really looked at the flower when he wrote this. In fact the Spanish missionaries in South America had seen the plant as a God-given symbol of the passion and of the ultimate triumph of the Cross. They used it in their conversion of the native Mexicans, teaching them to call it *'flor de las cinco llagas'* (flower of the five wounds), and nuns trained it round their cell windows. The plant was interpreted in one of two ways. In the first, the leaves were seen as the spear that pierced the side of Christ; the three stigmas, the nails of crucifixion; the five anthers, the five wounds; and the ten sepals, the disciples (Judas being absent for obvious reasons and Peter because of his denial of Christ). The second way is more detailed and I will use it later to lead me into meditation.

The Native American Houma tribe is known to have added passion flower extract to drinking water as a tonic. It became popular in the nineteenth century as a treatment for insomnia and was entered in the US National Formulary between 1916 and 1936. It does contain a non-addictive sedative that lowers blood pressure without causing drowsiness. Cut ripe fruits in autumn and cook for use in jams and puddings, or dry to make liquid medicinal infusions.
Note: Avoid in pregnancy.

Towards meditation

In my girlhood Good Friday was generally revered; no one worked, and the fishmonger opened briefly in the morning for the sale of cod and haddock, fresh from Grimsby that morning. The baker closed as soon as the last hot-cross bun had been sold. By noon the city had fallen silent and we would go to church to listen to a performance of Stainer's *Crucifixion*. In central London these days, even though most of the shops are open, I still detect a subdued atmosphere. Perhaps this is because of the concentration of churches there, all preparing in their different ways to commemorate the sufferings and death of Our Saviour. In rural France, there are generally fewer in the congregation than in England, and the 'Celebration of the Lord's Passion' at 3 o'clock has been cut to last no more than an hour. In our village, as I have mentioned, we have the liturgy only rarely, and I am usually obliged to observe Good Friday in my own solitary way. And that means heading gardenward again. The morning is a good time for planting potatoes, and the afternoon is perfect for training, layering and general care of the passion flower. It will not be in bloom yet, but one can envisage the flower in the mind's eye, or if the weather is inclement one can study a photograph indoors. After reading the liturgy, this is how I approached my meditation last Good Friday:

The passion flower and the Sorrowful Mysteries of the rosary
The agony in the garden
In the white of passion flower I saw the purity of Christ's obedience unto death as demonstrated by his prayer in the garden; in the violet, his sorrow and ours for our sin.

First decade of Hail Marys; meditation on Mark 14:32–42: 'They went to a place called Gethsemane.'

The scourging at the pillar
In the tendrils of passion flower I saw the cords that bound Jesus, the whips that bit into his flesh, and the reed with which they smote him; and, in the purple of the flowers, the robe they mockingly put upon him.

Second decade of Hail Marys; meditation on Mark 15:15: 'So Pilate, having scourged Jesus, delivered him to be crucified'; Mark 15:19: 'They struck his head with a reed'; and Mark 15:17a: 'They clothed him in a purple cloak.'

The crowning with thorns
The circle of filaments at the centre of the flower led me to imagine the agony of sharpness that pierced the head of Jesus and was symbolic to me of his mental torture, which is unimaginable.

Third decade of Hail Marys; meditation on Mark 15:17b: 'And plaiting a crown of thorns, they put it on him.'

Jesus carries his Cross
In the column of the ovary I saw the Cross itself, which the bleeding and weakened Jesus was forced to carry at least part of the way to Calvary, and I remembered the tradition that it was because he fell under its weight that Simon of Cyrene was made to carry it for him.

Fourth decade of Hail Marys; meditation on John 19:17: 'So they took Jesus, and he went out, bearing his own cross', and Luke 23:26: 'As they led him away, they seized one Simon of Cyrene, and laid on him the cross, to carry it behind Jesus.'

The crucifixion and death of Jesus
In the three stamens of the passion flower I saw the hammers and the nails of this most appalling method of execution; in the five anthers, the five wounds inflicted on the body of Christ.

Fifth decade of Hail Marys; meditation on Mark 15:26a: 'And they crucified him', and Mattthew 27:50: 'And Jesus cried again with a loud voice and yielded up his spirit.'

I came away from the meditation in a lather of horror, compassion, grief, shame, and desolation. But returning to the house it occurred to me that contemplation of the physical pain of the crucifixion must not stun me to the extent that I become incapable of reflection on its spiritual significance. Indoors I returned to Jeremiah 5: 'Remember, O Lord, what has befallen us; behold and see our disgrace!' and, at the end of Lamentations: 'Hast thou utterly rejected us? Art thou exceedingly angry with us?' Then it struck me forcibly that in Christ's own words from the Cross I would find the answers. The day was far spent, but there was time to list the relevant texts before preparing supper:
'Father, forgive them, for they know not what they do' (Luke 23:34);
'My God, my God, why has thou forsaken me?' (Matt. 27:46);
'Woman, behold your son' (John 19:26);
'Today you will be with me in Paradise' (Luke 23:43);
'I thirst' (John 19:28);
'It is finished' (John 19:30);
'Into thy hands I commit my spirit' (Luke 23:46).
Aware that each of these sayings is worthy of a lifetime's contemplation, and that together they encapsulate our Christian life-experience and hope, I put the list away, perhaps not until next Good Friday, although in the way of mortal things it probably will be. Later, just before sleep overwhelmed me, I remembered the legend that the life span of each *Passiflora* bloom is the same as the length of time between the burial and resurrection of Jesus.

Bible readings
Psalm 2: They take counsel against the Lord and his anointed.
Psalm 22: My God, my God , why hast thou forsaken me?
Psalm 31: In thee, O Lord, do I take refuge.

Isaiah 53: The prophet foresees the sufferings of the Servant Christ.
Hebrews 9:11–28: By the shedding of his blood Christ has entered the sanctuary.
1 Peter 1:18–19: You were ransomed with the precious blood of Christ.
1 John 1:7b: The blood of Jesus cleanses us from all sin.
1 Peter 2:21: Christ suffered for you, that you should follow in his steps.
And, if not present at the afternoon liturgy:
Isaiah 52:13–53: Behold my servant shall prosper.
Hebrews 4:14–16; 5:7–9: Being made perfect he became the source of eternal salvation.
Philippians 2:8–9: Therefore God has highly exalted him.
John 18 and 19: The passion.

Intercessions

For the grace of courage to follow Jesus to the Cross, today and everyday.
And, if not present at the afternoon liturgy:
For the Church, the pope, the clergy and laity; for those preparing for baptism; for Christian unity; for the Jewish people.

For those who do not believe in Christ; for those who do not believe in God; for all in public office; for those in special need.

Place of spiritual retreat

At the crucifixion and death of Jesus.

HOLY SATURDAY

ALOE VERA Barbados aloe; Curaçao aloe

Cultivation notes

Aloe vera is a tender evergreen perennial native to Socotra Island in the Indian Ocean. It is therefore necessary to make it feel at home by planting it in one-third sharp sand and two-thirds compost, and by maintaining a minimum temperature of $40°$ F. In these conditions it may attain a height of over a foot. The plant is naturally clump-forming and suckering, so to propagate remove offshoots in summer and dry for a couple of days before planting. Keep in sun or light shade and at all costs do not allow frost to touch it. It is amazingly drought resistant and therefore needs little water. The leaves are thick, spiky and greyish-green. Young plants sometimes have red-spotted leaves, and yellow flowers are occasionally borne in summer.

History and lore

For many centuries *aloe vera* grew only on Socotra, but it was eventually carried by Greek and Phoenician traders to their various ports of call. Later, the Portuguese took it farther afield, and it now grows in Africa, China, India and Central America. Greek physicians were using it as early as 400 BC. Oil of *aloe vera* was probably mixed with those of other aloe species, of which there are around 250, and used by the ancient Egyptians in their embalming process.

We know from John's Gospel that the Jews also used aloes in their burial practices. Nicodemus brought about a hundred pounds of aloes mixed with myrrh to help Joseph of Arimathea prepare the body of Jesus for the tomb. They were the first Christian undertakers. Aloe is mentioned in Anglo-Saxon sources as having been introduced to Europe in the tenth century. Although tender in our present European climate and normally grown as a houseplant, its history proves it remarkably resilient. Kept for long periods aboard sailing ships, it then survived long journeys by camel train and still rooted on replanting. The sap and leaves are remarkably effective in the soothing and healing of burns (including radiation burns), to the extent that, according to rumour among herbalists, several governments, that of the United States among them, have stockpiled it against nuclear accident or conflict. Aloe oil is widely used in the manufacture of many cosmetics, notably suntan lotions. It is a good idea to keep the plant in your kitchen, and then if someone has a burn or scald take a leaf, split it lengthwise and bind onto the affected skin with clean lint. The sap forms a clear protective seal that not only gives immediate relief from pain but also assists the healing process. Try not to rob the plant in winter when growth has slowed. It is best to buy a two-year-old plant because it is not advisable to use the leaves until the plant is of that age and well established. Application of aloe leaves is also good for fungal infections and eczema.

'Bitter aloes' is a preparation well known to erstwhile nail-biters. Smeared on the fingertips to discourage the habit by its bitter taste, it is made from the leaves of several aloe species. As well as using the fresh leaves you can try draining the sap and then evaporating it to a brown crystal for the preparation of skin creams, or as a scalp tonic in shampoos.

Note: Do not take aloe preparations internally except under qualified medical supervision.

Towards meditation

Looking back over the last few days, it is striking that so many plants have featured in the gospel narratives, and I have chosen aloe because it is one of the last two to have a connection with the earthly body of Our Lord. Holy Saturday (not Easter Saturday as many people mistakenly call it) is – on the surface – the most silent, empty, and desolate day of the Church's year. There is no Mass and the sacrament is given only to the dying. The Church is in the garden of Christ's tomb, holding herself still in a combination of grief and anticipation. And because we are her members, we are there with her, waiting and watching, while all around ask, 'Where is your God?'

In the Apostles' Creed we affirm that, between his death and resurrection, Christ descended into hell. This clause was not added until the fifth century and is based on the apocryphal gospel of Nicodemus, probably dating from the fourth century. This was popular throughout the medieval period, and there is a late Anglo-Saxon prose translation. William Langland includes it in *Piers Plowman*, and his work supplies some of the phrases in the York Mystery play of *The Harrowing of Hell*. Most notable of these is the scripturally based, *'Attolite porta ... introibit rex gloriae'* (Open gates, for the King of Glory is coming in). It is one of the most thrilling and satisfying moments in both poem and play:

> Dukes of this dark place
> Undo these gates so Christ come
> In, the son of heaven's King.
> With that word, hell split apart,
> Burst its devils bars; no man
> Nor guard could stop the gates swing
> Wide. The old religious men,
> Prophets, people who had walked
> In darkness, 'Behold the Lamb
> Of God', with Saint John sang now.

> But Lucifer could not look
> At it, the light blinding him.
> And along that light all those
> Our Lord loved came streaming out.[29]

But surely Christ did not need to go down into hell; he could have effected the release of all who had died between Adam and Eve and himself from anywhere he chose? It could be said that in his confronting hell he shared our human experience, but what is certain is that all the souls whom he loved had to be liberated. The gates of heaven were at last open to them because of Christ's redeeming sacrifice. Divine justice now demanded that the souls of Adam, Eve, the patriarchs, prophets and all the ordinary people who had sought God and loved him should be rescued and raised from darkness. Only Christ could do this rescuing and raising. That is why 'he descended into hell'. The second Office reading underlines the Church's belief. It is from an ancient homily for Holy Saturday that describes Christ's rescue of Adam from hell, and muses on Christ as the second Adam.

In common with many other Catholic beliefs, the descent into hell may be the result of our need to visualize divine action and truth, which of their nature must be invisible to us and on a level totally beyond our comprehension; so in our groping to understand and come nearer to God, we invent 'pictures'. But that gift of invention is from God in the first place, and as long as our imaginings have a sound theological base, as I believe this one does, then they do good rather than harm. And so, as we watch in grief and desolation by the garden tomb of Christ, we are able to bear his absence with equanimity, for we know that this is the anniversary of the raising to life eternal of our ancestors in faith, and that within a few hours we will celebrate again the fact that we too, through him, may inherit that life. And our knowledge of these things transforms Holy Saturday from a day of sorrow into a day of joy.

Bible readings

Psalm 64: Let the righteous rejoice in the Lord.
Psalm 30: Thou has brought up my soul from Sheol.
Hosea 6:1–3a: On the third day he will raise us up.
Hebrews 4:1–13: Today when you hear his voice, harden not your hearts.
1 John 2:1b–2: Jesus is the expiation ... for the sins of the whole world.
1 John 2:8b: The darkness is passing away.
John 19:38–42: Nicodemus came ... bearing a mixture of myrrh and aloes.

Intercessions

For those who govern, that responsible attitudes and actions may prevail in the management of nuclear power; for all who have been disfigured by burns, and for those recovering from such injuries, for fire-fighters, and for those they have been unable to save; for sufferers from skin cancer; for medical staff who care for victims of fire or skin disease; and for those researching new treatments for their patients.

For those whose discipleship is secret because of persecution, and for those who suffer because of their faith; for all who mourn; for undertakers; for those who cannot be given funerals according to their faith; for the 'disappeared' and their families.

That the Lent we have made may be acceptable to God, and that we may wait in thanksgiving and serenity until the celebration of Christ's resurrection.

Place of spiritual retreat

In the garden of Christ's burial, as in John 19.

THE EASTER VIGIL

EASTER LILY *Lilium longiflorum*
ARUM LILY *Zantedeschia aethipica*

Cultivation notes

Although the daffodil is sometimes called the Lent or Easter lily, *Lilium longiflorum* is the true Easter lily. The arum lily is included as it is found in many churches at Easter. In Britain both do best as house, conservatory or greenhouse plants. Only in warmer climates should they be attempted outdoors, and even then they should be reared under glass and planted in the open only when the spring mornings are safely frost free.

Lilium longiflorum is probably the most popular for growing indoors. It can reach a height of three feet and produces white flower trumpets with pale-yellow centres. These can be up to six inches long and are valued for the sweetness of their scent. Summer is their natural flowering time, so they have to be forced in time for Easter. In autumn buy a plump unshrivelled bulb and plant straightaway in a 6–10 inch pot. Submerge the tip under about 1½ inches of compost. Put in a dark, cold place (but not less than 35°F), and keep the compost moist throughout cultivation. Move into bright light, but not direct sun, when the bulb begins to shoot. Do not let the temperature exceed 50°F during the growing period. Continue to keep the soil moist and mist the leaves occasionally. After flowering reduce watering, but do not allow to dry out. Repot in autumn and expect smaller flowers next year.

Arum lilies grow from rhizomes. The pure white flowers, which can be up to nine inches in length, appear from early spring to June, and are spathes furled around a single wand-like golden stamen. The plant needs a temperature of 50° and can reach a height of three feet. Keep dry in winter; water well at other times. Propagate by dividing rhizomes from October to January.

History and lore

According to scholars, neither of today's lilies is mentioned in the Bible. The ones in the Song of Solomon 2:2 are believed to have been Madonna lilies (see the Annunciation, 25 March); as for the lilies of the field referred to by Jesus in Matthew 6:28, it is generally held that he was using a generic term for any beautiful wild flower or that he was thinking of the scarlet-purple *Anemone coronaria*, which, growing in a large swathe, could be said to surpass 'Solomon in all his glory'. Any kind of white lily has come to symbolize a person of unsullied purity. For us there are only two such, namely, Jesus himself and his blessed Mother, with whom the Madonna lily has been inextricably associated in Christian art down the centuries. But on the day we celebrate the resurrection of the Spotless Lamb, there could surely be no more appropriate flowers than the two fragrant lilies I have chosen. Although the arum lily is not the true Easter lily, horticulturally speaking, it perhaps has the edge over *Lilium longiflorum* because of two ancient traditions. The first is that as Eve left the Garden of Eden she shed tears, not just because of her banishment but also as an expression of real repentance, and from those tears grew arum lilies. (Some versions of this legend claim this distinction for Madonna lilies.) The spiritual lesson to be drawn is that from genuine repentance come grace and the beginnings of true beauty. The second legend is that arum lilies really ought to be called Gethsemane lilies because they were found in the garden after our Lord's agony there. From the places on the ground where his sweat had fallen the exquisite flowers sprang to life, as he himself would do in a beauty surpassing that of everything else in his creation.

Towards meditation

During my long years as a chorister, we used to call the Sacred Triduum 'the marathon'. (We were in exalted company, for St Paul uses the same image, although he was of course referring to the whole spiritual race of life, not just to three days at the end of Holy Week.) Falling into bed on Maundy Thursday, I would comfort myself with the motto, 'They who sing pray twice', and commit to God a weekend during which there would be very little time for private prayer. After the Easter Vigil, there was a collective 'hitting of the wall' before we returned to sing the High Mass of Easter Day. Unless you have been through this you cannot have an inkling of what is experienced in a choir gallery of believing Catholics during the Triduum. And if, as a listener, you do, then the choir has not done its job properly, for it must support the liturgy without self-indulgent emotionalism and, moreover, sing some of the most beautiful and at times complex music in the Church's treasury. I still miss it but am grateful that release from this form of serving has enabled me to enter another of increasing depth as the years pass. In a way I have been on retreat since I lost my voice.

As the sun sets on Holy Saturday, together with millions of my brothers and sisters, I prepare for the 'mother of all vigils', as St Augustine called the Easter vigil. Every year the new fire of Easter is struck from flint; every year the paschal candle is lit from it and set up in sanctuaries across the world; every year the darkness is vanquished as the candle comes into church and we light our own tapers from it. Both fire and candle signify Christ's resurrection, and as God went before the Israelites in a pillar of fire to light their way in darkness so Christ goes symbolically before us in the form of the paschal candle. It is incredibly stirring for us who believe, but would that we could do more to take the light of Christ out into the world that so desperately needs it! But however much I am affected by the drama of the Easter vigil as a whole, however much I am moved by the sight of the catechumens coming forward for baptism, it is the *Exultet* that increasingly arrests me as the years pass. The full and proper singing of this hymn takes about 18 minutes. Its authorship is unknown, although it has been attributed to both Augustine and Ambrose of Milan. Scholarship dates it to the fifth century, but the chant has a much earlier feel, and I am always overcome with the sensation that the lone voice of the deacon in the candlelit cavern of the church is not his voice at all but that of one of the earliest apostles, perhaps even of Paul or Peter themselves. Words fail at this perception.

The *Exultet* falls into five sections:

1. An invitation to joy and thanksgiving, followed by the humble prayer of the cantor that he may sing worthily in praise of the paschal candle, symbolic of the risen Jesus. Then follows a short dialogue with the people, as normally precedes the preface at Mass.
2. Praise and thanksgiving to God for his redemptive work.
3. Types and figures from the Old Testament are recalled: the paschal lamb; the passage through the Red Sea; God going before the people in a pillar of fire.
4. The five (in the original Latin) 'O's' section of awestruck and awe-inspiring reverence for the night on which the splendour of our redemption was wrought.
5. Prayer that God will accept our tribute and that the paschal candle, symbolically the risen Christ, may shine and never be extinguished.

Most people do not have the chance to hear the 'O' section as it was originally written, and because it is such a rich source for meditation it is given here in the translation from the pre-conciliar *Saint Andrew Daily Missal:*

> O wonderful condescension of your mercy towards us!
> O inestimable affection of charity: that you might redeem a slave, you delivered up your Son!
> O truly needful sin of Adam, which was blotted out by the death of Christ!
> O happy fault that merited so great a redeemer!
> O truly blessed night, which alone deserved to know the time and the hour in which Christ rose again from the grave: this is the night of which it is written: 'And the night shall be enlightened as the day; and the night is my light in my enjoyments. Therefore, the holiness of this night drives away all wickedness, cleanses faults, and restores innocence to the fallen, and gladness to the sorrowful. It puts to flight hatred, brings peace and humbles pride.'

And so the vigil moves on through the Liturgy of the Word until it reaches the gospel, which is the resurrection account from one of the synoptic evangelists, depending on the three-year cycle. They conflict slightly in their detail, but all three make it clear that women were the first to discover the empty tomb. John's account, which is not included in the cycle, has Mary Magdalene going alone to the tomb early in the morning and finding the stone rolled back. She runs to tell Peter and John, who come and look into the tomb and then return to their homes, while Mary stays outside the tomb, weeping. And then she sees Jesus, but she does not recognize him until he speaks her name. Afterwards, she goes to the disciples and tells them that she has 'seen the Lord'. John's version is the foundation of the wonderful sequence *Victimae paschali laudes*. But that is for tomorrow. My Easter joy is deepened by the privileged role women played in the events following the resurrection of Jesus. Whether or not Mary Magdalene had the honour of seeing him first for all of us, women *and* men, I most fervently desire to stay with her, and to meditate in the remaining hours of darkness after the vigil, on 'Rabboni', her word of recognition to him. And so I conclude, at the dawn of Easter Day, in the garden of the Resurrection of Jesus Christ our Saviour and Redeemer, praying that he will call us all by name, and that we shall recognize him.

Bible readings
If not attending the vigil, readings from its Liturgy of the Word.

Place of spiritual retreat
With Mary Magdalene on Easter morning, as in John 20.

Part 2

Solemnities and Saints' Days

SOLEMNITIES AND SAINTS' DAYS

INTRODUCTORY NOTE

This volume is written as if Lent has begun after 11 March. Saints whose days occur if Lent starts at its earliest date have full entries in *Gardening with God: Light in Darkness*. I treat fully below of the two Solemnities, St Joseph and the Annunciation, of the feast of St Mark, and of the Memorial of St John Baptist de la Salle. Other saints whose days occur between 15 March and 23 April have only an optional memorial or commemoration. Of these I have included SS Patrick, Anselm and George. For the others I would suggest as follows:

18 March: Cyril of Jerusalem, bishop and doctor (315–86): Jerusalem artichoke
23 March: Turibius of Mogrovejo, bishop (1538–1606): Peruvian bark
2 April: Francis of Paola, hermit and patron of seafarers (1416–1507): kelp
4 April: Isidore of Seville, bishop and doctor (c. 560–636): Seville orange
5 April: Vincent Ferrer, priest (1350–1419): oxslip
11 April: Stanislaus of Cracow, bishop and martyr (1030–79): hop
13 April: Martin I, pope and martyr (d. 655): love-lies-bleeding
24 April: Fidelis of Sigmaringen, priest and martyr (1528–1622): tulip 'Fidelio'

St Louise de Marillac begins this section because of my own Vincentian background, and because she is a wonderful example of charity, prayer and self-denial. It would therefore be strange to omit her from a Lenten book.

MARCH

15 MARCH
St Louise de Marillac, widow (1591–1660)

POTATO *Solanum tuberosum*

Cultivation notes

The reputation of the potato for cleaning ground is really due not to some innate property in the plant but to the amount of weeding that has to be done at every stage of growth: first during the digging of the plot, making trenches and setting the seed; then with each successive earthing-up; and finally when the crop is lifted. Furthermore, the whole process vastly improves the friability of the soil. The best size for planting is that of a hen's egg. If they are not already sprouting, 'chit' seed-potatoes in egg-boxes in a cool frost-free place, well lit but not in direct sun. Ideal planting time is when the sprouts from the 'eyes' are about an inch long. In Devon I used to allocate enough of my quarter acre to provide main crop potatoes throughout the winter. These were stored in large black refuse bins, layered with newspaper, and checked every so often to make sure none had rotted. When I came back to London it took me a long time to overcome resentment at having to buy potatoes. In France, the year of writing this book was the first time I tried them again after the red bug plague that attacked my crop in the mid-1990s.

On Good Friday morning I put in seven rows of 'Belle de Fontenay', classified in France as early or second early. The patch had been green-manured with alfalfa during the previous season, and by early June the haulms had reached a height of eight inches to a foot above the second earthing-up. I did not feed them, as too much fertilizer can lead to overproduction of foliage at the expense of yield. We were set fair to enjoy home-grown new potatoes throughout the long summer holidays.

In England popular earlies are the kidney-shaped 'Duke of York', the oval, waxy 'Pentland Javelin', the oval 'Sutton Foremost' and the round 'Epicure'. Maincrop favourites are the oval, waxy yellow-fleshed 'Desirée' and the high-yielding, well-flavoured 'Maris Piper'. 'Pentland Javelin' and 'Desirée' are good for French potato dishes, but for general cooking

154

versatility, flavour, high yield and storage tolerance the white-fleshed 'Pentland Crown' and 'Pentland Ivory' have always been my choice for maincrop. If storing, reject any that show signs of pest, disease or damage. Do not store potatoes with skins that can be rubbed off. Keep in a cool, dry place well away from frost. Try to ensure that all tubers have been got up from the soil. If left in the ground they can encourage disease and pests.

History and lore

The word 'potato' comes from the Spanish *patata*, which in its turn comes from the native name *batata* in Haiti. There is no hard evidence for the commonly heard claim that it was introduced to Britain by Sir John Hawkins or Sir Walter Ralegh. However, according to Maggie Campbell-Culver in *The Origin of Plants*,[1] it is possible that it may have been brought from Chile in 1586 by Thomas Heriot, a botanist who sailed with Sir Francis Drake. Originally it was grown in Europe as cattle-fodder, and perhaps for that reason was looked down upon. Some people refused to eat it because it is not mentioned in the Bible. By 1904, however, it was so well established that the redoubtable Sutton and Sons referred to it in *The Culture of Vegetables and Flowers* (1904) as 'the king of the kitchen garden'. There was also for a time the slang idiom 'the potato', meaning the best, the tip-top or the correct thing.

Until I lived in Devon I had not heard of the custom of setting seed-potatoes on Good Friday, but there I discovered the saying, 'Uz plants uz taddies at the foot of the cross'. The belief was that peas and beans planted at the same time would also flourish, because on the anniversary of the crucifixion the devil's power over the earth is vanquished. In *Folklore and Customs of Rural England*, Margaret Baker reports that in 1955 a Surrey gardener was offered time off on Easter weekend. He refused, explaining to his employer that he wanted to sow seed on Holy Saturday, 'while the Master's body lay on the ground'.

The potato has the traditional meaning of benevolence, and it is chosen for Louise de Marillac because she was an aristocrat who embraced poverty, humility and works of charity. She was diligent in the service of the poor, as indeed the potato has been for centuries, in providing them with a diet staple. By the time she was 15 Louise had lost both parents. After considering religious life, she married Antoine le Gras. They lived happily and had one son, but Antoine died in 1625, when Louise was only 34 years of age. Then free to devote herself entirely to God, she was uncertain as to how, until she met St Vincent de Paul. He became her spiritual director, and later with him she founded the Daughters of Charity, who would become one of the largest religious orders in the world. St Vincent does not appear to have specifically intended to found a religious institute, and he said to the early companions of Louise, 'Your convent will be the house of the sick, your cell a rented room, your chapel the parish church, your cloister the city streets and hospital corridors, your enclosure obedience, your grille fear of God, your veil modesty.' They took no vows until 1642, and then only for a year at a time. Louise de Marillac was canonized in 1934.

For over three centuries her daughters were distinguished by their graceful grey-blue habit and large, wing-like, starched linen *cornette*, worn in place of a veil. It was based on the traditional dress of Breton peasant women of the seventeenth century. I was teaching in a Vincentian school on the day in 1964 when the Sisters replaced the habit with three-quarter-length skirts, blouses and cardigans, and their *cornettes* with skimpy blue veils that showed their hair. We lay teachers thought it was a disaster and could not believe that any of the Sisters enjoyed the change – except perhaps the community laundresses. But whatever the Sisters felt, they made no comment and went about the day as if nothing had happened. Like their foundress, they had embraced plain poverty and humility. There was no room for vanity. In their lives of self-effacement and active love of the poor and sick they were fruitful seed in the Lord's garden. They were not, like Chaucer's prioress, concerned with the effect their appearance might have on others. Nevertheless, I think that, before the modernization of their habits, religious Sisters were afforded proper respect for what they were and did. Something of great value went from the streets of Sheffield, and every city, after the *cornette* was lost. Whereas before, the descendants of St Louise shone out as beacons, bringing Christ's love to the darkest and poorest of places, ever since 1964 they have scurried about like the rest of us, hardly distinguishable in the crazy Christlessness of urban desperation.

On or around St Louise's day, when I buy my seed-potatoes, I remember with gratitude and love Sister Agnes, who brought me into the faith. As I set the seed to 'chit' I commit to God all city-dwellers, particularly those who reject him or do not know him; every time I inspect the length of the sprouts from the 'eyes' I ask the Holy Spirit for grace, that I may grow in humility and love; digging the trenches, I offer all my gardening and domestic work to Christ; setting the seed, my prayer to the Holy Trinity asks for strength, truth and creativity in my teaching and writing and will conclude with thanksgiving for grace already bestowed; with each earthing-up I ask for God's continued protection; and at crop-lifting, I ask to go at last to meet Christ, bearing fruits acceptable to him.

Bible readings
Job 30:25: Did I not weep for him whose day was hard? Was not my grief for the poor?
Job 31:18: I reared him as a father, and from his mother's womb I guided him.
Psalm 41:1: Blessed is he who considers the poor.
Isaiah 58:7–11: Share your bread with the hungry.
Sirach 29:12: Store up almsgiving in your treasury.
Tobit 4:16: Give your bread to the hungry, and your clothing to the naked.
Matthew 25:31–46: As you did it to the least of these my brethren, you did it to me.

Intercessions
For Daughters of Charity throughout the world.

Place of spiritual retreat
Listening to Jesus' teaching, as in Matthew 25.

17 MARCH
St Patrick, bishop, patron of Ireland (c. 385–c. 461)

LESSER TREFOIL *Trifolium dubium*; Shamrock
WHITE CLOVER *Trifolium repens*[2]

Cultivation notes
The identity of the trifoliate plant supposedly used by Patrick to expound the doctrine of the Trinity is shrouded in mystery. The word 'shamrock' comes from the Irish '*seamrog*' and means 'little clover', and lesser trefoil is the plant usually worn by the Irish to celebrate their national day. It is probably the most common hop trefoil, named thus because its brown fruit heads look like the heads of minute hops, and 'lesser' because it is smaller than its relative, *Trifolium campestre*. Other plants that have been suggested as the true shamrock are white clover, black medick and wood sorrel. Black

---

medick and lesser trefoil can be confused when in flower, but the former has a point at the tip of each leaf. The difference becomes very clear once seedheads appear. The flowers of medick drop off to show black pods, whereas the flowers of the trefoil do not fall but cover straight brown pods. I have some black medick seeds from the HDRA organic catalogue[3] and hope to celebrate St Patrick's day next year with this alternative 'shamrock'.

History and lore

The Patrick who expelled all the snakes from Ireland and singlehandedly achieved the conversion of that country is now known to be a figment of legend. The only authentic facts about him are to be found in his writings, which were the first to spring from the British Church. These are his autobiography (*Confession*), his letter against slave-trading written to Coroticus; and 'St Patrick's Breastplate', subsequently adapted as a hymn. The words of this last make it unthinkable to celebrate his day with anything other than a trifoliate plant.

Patrick was born in the west of England at a place called Bannavem Taburniam. His father was a deacon and his grandfather a priest. As a youth he was captured by pirates and taken to Ireland, where he remained for six years as a herdsman in slavery. During this time he began to pray, which he had not done before his capture. Eventually he escaped, or was released, and persuaded some sailors to take him to England. After much hardship, he returned to his family and received a rudimentary education and training for the priesthood. He knew the Latin Bible, but he was never a scholar and remained conscious of this to the end of his long life. He had contact with Gaul and is now one of the patrons of France, together with Denis, Joan of Arc and King Louis IX. Pope Celestine I had sent Palladius to be the first bishop of Ireland. Patrick was appointed his successor and returned to Ireland in about 435. He worked mainly in the north and set up various sees. He had a school and from it made his many missionary journeys. The place of Patrick's death and burial is uncertain, although Lérins (France), Croagh Patrick and Downpatrick (Ireland) all claim the distinction, while Glastonbury (England) may have some of his relics.

Towards meditation

The second Office reading is an extract from Patrick's *Confession*. It is refreshing to read each year because it dispels the image of the popular wonderworker, makes one realize how many problems he faced, and so transforms him from a remote figure encrusted with unlikely legend into living flesh, blood and spirit.

First Patrick thanks God for his faith, gladly making an offering of his life to Christ, who he believes has kept him safe through all the troubles and dangers he has endured. Humbly he asks, 'Who am I Lord, and what is my calling that you should cooperate with me in such divine power?' Among the pagans, whether things go well or badly, he praises and proclaims the name of the Lord wherever he goes. Even in stress he thanks God because he trusts him without reserve. In spite of Patrick's acknowledged ignorance, God has inspired him and enabled him to carry out his mission successfully and to imitate, in a small way, the apostles whom Christ predicted would carry the Good News to all nations before the world ends. Patrick goes on to question in wonder how he came by wisdom when he knew nothing. How did he come to be given the marvellous gift of loving and knowing God, to the extent of leaving his home and family? Among the Irish pagans he has been insulted and his mission abused; he has been persecuted and put in chains. He has given up his freedom for the sake of others and would be willing, if found worthy, to undergo martyrdom. If it is God's will, he wishes to stay in Ireland until he dies. Towards the close of the extract Patrick owns his debt to God for the grace of being able to convert souls and to be instrumental in bringing so many to ordination from among his flock.

In the garden, because I have no shamrock as yet, I contemplate one of my clover paths, and as I pray the opening verses of 'St Patrick's Breastplate' feel myself encouraged, bolstered and protected by the strength of his personality and faith:

> I bind unto myself today
> The strong name of the Trinity:
> By invocation of the same,
> The Three in One and One in Three.
>
> I bind this day to me for ever,
> By power of faith, Christ's incarnation,
> His baptism in the Jordan River,
> His death on the Cross for my salvation,
> His bursting from the spiced tomb,
> His riding up the heavenly way,
> His coming at the day of doom
> I bind unto myself today.[4]

Bible readings
Jeremiah 1:4–9: To all to whom I send you, you shall go.
Psalm 117: Great is his steadfast love toward us.
Acts 13:46–9: I have set you to be a light for the Gentiles.
1 Thessalonians 2:1–11, 19–26: Remember our labours among you.
Hebrews 13:7–9: Remember your leaders who spoke to you of the word of God.
1 Timothy 4:16: Take heed to your teaching.
1 Timothy 5:17–22; 6:10–14: Let the elders be considered worthy of double honour.
Luke 4:18–19: He has anointed me to preach good news to the poor.
Luke 10:1–12, 17-20: After this the Lord appointed 70 others.

Intercessions
For the people of Ireland and France.
    For bishops, pastors and missionaries.

Place of spiritual retreat
Among the 70 sent out by Christ, as in Luke 10.

19 MARCH: SOLEMNITY
St Joseph, husband of the Blessed Virgin Mary

COMMON ASH *Fraxinus excelsior*
WEEPING ASH *F. excelsior*; 'Pendula'

Cultivation notes
The common ash can
grow to a height of 130 feet.
Male and female flowers
are often present on the
same tree, giving it a
purple colour before the
appearance of the leaves. It is a
forest tree, so unless you own woodland its
symbolism in the garden is best achieved
by growing the weeping *F. excelsior* 'Pendula'
or the manna ash.

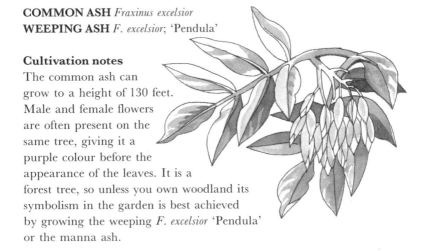

History and lore

The ash is native to Europe, western Asia and North Africa. Its English name derives from the Anglo-Saxon *aesc*, and *fraxinus* from the Latin for a spear or javelin with an ash-wood shaft. *Excelsior*, the 'comparative' of the Latin *excelsus*, meaning high or lofty, may seem an obvious description for such a tall tree, but there is perhaps a deeper reason that has origins in pagan lore. Before the advent of Christianity the ash was worshipped as a symbol of life. Odin was believed to have carved the first man out of ash wood. Yggdrasil, the 'Tree of the World', was a giant ash whose roots reached down to the lowest depths of hell and whose crown grew so tall that it reached heaven, with its mighty trunk connecting the two. In English lore witches were supposed to fear the ash, and so it was chosen to make milk pails and the handles of threshing flails. It was thought that sick children could be cured by passing them through the cleft of an ash, and droving sticks made from ash wood were believed incapable of causing injury to cattle. The tradition that interests me most is the peculiarly Devonian one of burning an 'ashen faggot' as a Yule log. This had to be bound with nine withies and lit with a charred twig from the embers of the previous year's Christmas Eve hearth. Margaret Baker records in *Folklore and Customs of Rural England* that in 1878 the Devon Association reported Christmas ash faggots ablaze in 32 dwellings in the Ashburton area alone. A century later I lived within 15 miles of Ashburton and never saw one bound in the proper way. However, wood for the Christmas fire was always chosen with great care, and huge logs crackled in the grates of most local houses and inns. My cousin-in-law at Widecombe always bore a prize log into the house with great ceremony.

Ash-wood is white, coarse-grained, extremely strong and durable, and is still used to make oars and tool handles. William Coles claimed that three or four leaves taken in wine each morning 'doth make those leane that are fat', and said that the ashes of the bark cured 'leprous, scabby or scal'd heads'. Modern herbalists recommend an infusion of ash leaves – half a cup of ash leaves to 2½ cups of boiling water taken over 24 hours – as an effective laxative that is gentler than senna. Ash is said to have anti-inflammatory properties and was formerly used to treat rheumatism and arthritis.

There is one biblical reference to the ash, in Isaiah 44:14. Many authorities believe, in spite of its availability, that this tree, used for carving idols, was not the ash at all but one of a variety of conifers. The Syrian ash (*Fraxinus syriaca*) grew, and still grows, in the Holy Land. It is

161

not as tall as its European relative but shares its other qualities. I like to think that St Joseph would have known, appreciated and used it in his workshop, and perhaps even had a walking staff made from it. To make an ash stick, treat in exactly the same way as hazel (see p. 103). Whereas the hazel stick will be coppery, the ash stick will have a silvery-grey patina.

History and lore of St Joseph

The tradition that Joseph was an old man at the time of Jesus' birth has its origins in the apocryphal *Protevangelium of James*. The Greek *History of Joseph the Carpenter* (fifth or sixth century) is thought to have been instrumental in creating his cult, and in England his feast was celebrated before 1100 in the cathedral cities of Winchester, Worcester and Ely. Bridget of Sweden (1303–73), Vincent Ferrer (1350–1419) and Bernadino of Siena (1380–1444) all encouraged devotion to him, possibly as an antidote to his presentation as a comic butt in the medieval Mystery plays. However, having adapted and directed some of these plays, I have found that they allow a deeply spiritual and poignant interpretation of Joseph's character and predicament. His feast seems to have been celebrated on 19 March since the fifteenth century and was supported by no less than Ignatius of Loyola (1491–1536). The Roman missal of 1503 includes his feast, as do Carmelite Office books of 1480, and possibly the greatest impetus in the development of devotion to St Joseph came from St Teresa of Avila (1513–82), who dedicated her reformed Carmelite motherhouse to him and mentioned him frequently in her writings, saying that she knew from experience that he helped 'in every need'. In 1621 Gregory XV added the feast to the Universal Calendar; in 1714 Clement XI composed a new Office; in 1847 Pius IX declared him 'Patron of the Universal Church'; and in 1962 John XXIII added his name to the Canon of the Mass. European devotion to St Joseph has therefore been constant for almost a thousand years. Not surprisingly, Joseph is the patron of fathers, bursars and carpenters, but perhaps most notably of the dying and of all who wish to die a holy death. This last patronage probably has its roots in the *History of Joseph the Carpenter*, which includes an imagined account of Joseph's fear of death. Wracked by self-criticism, he is comforted by Mary and by Jesus, who promises protection and life to all who do good works in the name of his foster-father. This legend may explain the vast number of schools, parishes, hospitals and religious institutes that have taken Joseph as their patron.

Towards meditation

The second Office reading is from Sermon 2 on St Joseph by the great Franciscan preacher Bernardino of Siena, and it is helpful on the day of such an important saint about whom we know so little. The extract opens with the claim that whenever God wishes to impart his grace to a person, or select him for a particular honour, he gives him all the gifts needed to sustain him in the demands of that calling. This seems especially true of Joseph. Bernardino has faith that Jesus would have especially kept his promise in the case of his foster-father and said to him after death, 'Good and faithful servant, enter into the joy of your Lord.' (At this point I have an annual twinge of poignant recollection that, as Joseph probably died before Jesus, he would have been among those Our Lord loved and led to the light from the darkness of hell. Perhaps the roots of Joseph's legendary fear of death lie in this.) Next we are reminded that the Church owes a great debt to Mary, because through her cooperation with God the Father, God the Son was able to enter into the world through the action of God the Holy Spirit. We owe Joseph special thanks and reverence too, because he played his part in bringing up the child Jesus to manhood and prepared him to go out into the world. In Joseph the integrity of the patriarchs and prophets is vindicated, and he had the amazing privilege of seeing in the flesh the Messiah that God had promised to them. We know from Luke's Gospel that Jesus was obedient to Joseph and paid him the honour and respect due from a son to his earthly father. Again Bernardino has faith that in heaven Christ will have transformed, completed and perfected his relationship with Joseph. In the light of this, Joseph, the carpenter, husband of the Virgin Mary, must be a powerful intercessor for us with Christ, to whom Bernardino appeals at the close of the Office excerpt.

Reading Bernardino makes me think that the little we know of Joseph is actually a great deal, for in him, on a very human level, are the lessons we should learn about doubt, obedience, love, service and responsible love and protection of those in our charge.

Bible readings

2 Samuel 7:4–5, 12–14, 17: Your house and your kingdom shall be made sure.

Psalm 89: His line shall endure for ever.

Proverbs 2:7–8: He is a shield to those who walk in integrity.

Wisdom of Solomon 10:10: When a righteous man fled from his brother's wrath.

Colossians 3:23–4: Whatever your task, work heartily, as serving the Lord not men.

Hebrew 11:1–16: These all died in faith, not having received what was promised.

Luke 12:42: The faithful and wise steward, whom his master will set over his household.

Matthew 1:16–24: Joseph, son of David, do not fear to take Mary your wife.

Matthew 25:21: Well done, good and faithful servant.

Luke 2:41–51: He went down with them to Nazareth, and was obedient unto them.

Intercessions

For the people of Devon, Hampshire, Worcestershire and Cambridgeshire.

For carpenters, wood-carvers, and manual workers; for natural, adoptive and foster-fathers; for all institutions under the patronage of St Joseph.

Thanksgiving for the life and writings of Bernardino of Siena, Teresa of Avila and of all the saints and Fathers.

For those who fear death.

Thanksgiving for the lessons to be learned from the role of St Joseph, and that we may appeal to his intercession; for grace to live our lives in such a way that we may at last hear Christ say to us, 'Good and faithful servant, enter into the joy of your Lord.'

Place of spiritual retreat

In the house at Nazareth, as in Luke 2.

25 MARCH: SOLEMNITY
The Annunciation of the Lord

MADONNA LILY *Lilium candidum*

Cultivation notes

This perennial bulb produces stems that can reach a height of five feet. They have three-inch leaves all the way up to the flower clusters of five to twenty glistening white blooms. These are yellow at the internal base and appear in summer. Popular for their tall elegance and sweet scent, Madonna lilies are hardy and appreciate a sunny position in well-drained soil. Choose their site carefully because they do not like transplantation and will flower only in the correct conditions. Plant the bulbs in autumn no deeper than two inches below the surface. They tend to be expensive – perhaps about £3 each. Once the first plantation is established, try raising seed sown under cover in autumn, plant stem-scales in summer or offsets towards the beginning of autumn. If required for medical use, pick flowers as they open and lift bulbs in autumn. Bulbs can be frozen until needed.

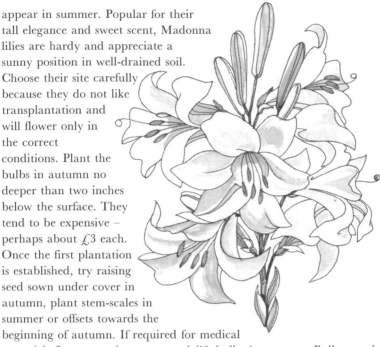

History and lore

The Madonna lily is native to the eastern Mediterranean area and was probably introduced to Britain by the Romans. The word 'Madonna' was not added until the nineteenth century, to distinguish the plant from many other lilies being introduced at the time. *Candidum* means a glistening, shining white and is in keeping with the legend that the Madonna and not the Arum lily sprang from the tears of Eve as she said goodbye to Paradise. From the early days of Christianity it was dedicated to the Virgin Mary (the second Eve), no doubt because of the purity of its flowers and sweet fragrance. Another legend has it that when St Thomas doubted that the Virgin had been assumed bodily into heaven, her opened tomb was found to contain only lilies and roses. The Madonna lily features in many paintings of the Annunciation, where it is held by the Archangel Gabriel or placed in a vase elsewhere in the picture. Pre-Reformation public houses named The Angel would have had an inn sign depicting the

Annunciation, but with the onset of Puritanism Our Lady was painted out, as being a papist symbol. Eventually Gabriel had to go as well, leaving only the lily. In one case, according to Mark Elvins in *Catholic Trivia*,[5] even the flower went, and the pub was renamed The Flowerpot! There was a public house in London's Islington that retained the angel on its sign, hence the name of the district and the Underground station.

Florentine artists often featured the lily because it had been incorporated into their city coat of arms as a symbol of the Blessed Virgin, the patroness of Florence. Earlier, the fleur-de-lys had become the emblem of France because during the reign of Clovis (465–511) an angel was said to have appeared to a hermit, holding in his hand a shield emblazoned with three gold lilies. He commanded the hermit to give this to Clovis's wife, Queen Clothilde, who had embraced Christianity. After the hermit had carried out the angel's order, Clovis adopted the emblem and was then everywhere victorious. English lore holds that the Madonna lily will grow only for a good woman and that its holy aura keeps malign influences away from her dwelling. And corn will be plentiful and cheap in a year when the lily blooms well.

The Madonna lily has a long medicinal history and is mentioned by Pliny, who describes its use as a cure for skin troubles and foot problems. It is not much used today, probably because there are other, cheaper, herbs that have similar effects. However, the bulbs and flowers were once used to treat burns, abscesses, chilblains, ulcers and even alopecia. It is now known that its astringent properties do have the power to heal damaged skin.

As I write, my own Madonna lilies, given to me by a retired Parisian fireman, are in bloom, probably for the first time since 1996. That year, and indeed this, they afforded a second little annunciation.

History of the Annunciation in the Church

We do not know the exact date when the Church began to celebrate the Annunciation, and it is generally supposed that the date in March was chosen because it is nine months before Christmas. However, Benedict XIV argued that the date was known in ancient tradition to have been the actual day of the event, and St Augustine in his fourth book on the Trinity refers to such a tradition.[6] The same day is mentioned in Greek, Syrian, Coptic and Chaldean calendars and martyrologies, as well as in the *Sacramentary* of St Gregory. Apart from Augustine's reference, mention was made of it at the Council of Trullo (692) and in the homilies attributed to

166

Gregory the Wonderworker (c. 213–c. 270). Listed in the pre-Vatican II missal as a feast of the Blessed Virgin, it is now 'The Annunciation of the Lord', which is indeed more accurate since it is Christ whom the angel announces, and not his mother-to-be.

Towards meditation

During Advent I promised to observe today's solemnity by meditating on two frescoes, one by Fra Angelico and the other by an unknown nineteenth-century artist in the apse of my London church. However, on reflection, since the latter is not generally known or accessible, I have decided to look at well-known representations of the mystery that seem to me to depict the different mental and spiritual states through which Mary passed during Gabriel's visit. In the fifteenth century these were divided into her agitation, reflection, enquiry and submission. Botticelli's painting (c. 1489/90), whilst it in no way suggests agitation, does seem to me to catch the moment before Mary made her wholehearted *Fiat*. She is standing, although seemingly about to sink into a faint, with her head bent and her eyes downcast. Her face is submissive and accepting, but there is a hesitancy conveyed by her hands, which creates a certain ambiguity. Gabriel looks up at her with an expression of wondering expectation, as if he is not quite certain what her decision will be. He holds the lily in his left hand, and Botticelli has perfectly positioned it so that its blooms show above his head and are on a level with Mary's heart. His hand, too, reaches out. But the figures do not touch and are divided by the door jamb in the background. Beyond and behind Gabriel is an open landscape, but Mary is hidden in the room, perhaps symbolizing her purity and separation from the normal run of humanity. The distance between the hands of Mary and Gabriel seems to me the central point of the painting, conveying the tension of the moment just before the Incarnation was assured.

Another favourite of mine is the panel painting by Fra Filippo Lippi (c. 1406–69). Here I see the moments after the conception of Christ, with the heads of both Gabriel and Mary bowed in contemplative prayer. Gabriel is kneeling and Mary is seated, but there is perfect grace and balance between them. Mary's hand is laid gently against her ribcage, and the Holy Spirit in the form of a dove rests above the two figures in Mary's half of the painting. She and Gabriel are separated by a low balustrade, on which stands a pot of lilies. Mary is indoors and Gabriel in the garden, also holding lilies.

Turning now to Fra Angelico (c. 1387–1455), we find Mary and Gabriel again separated, this time by the central pillar of a loggia that resembles the cloister of the artist's monastery. Yet again Mary is inside the building, and other inner rooms, depicted in masterly perspective, stretch behind her. Gabriel has stepped through the archways from the garden outside. He is bending a knee in apparent reverence; she is seated and on a slightly higher level. To me the fresco depicts a later moment in the mystery than the Botticelli painting. Sometimes I see a waiting stillness in it, created to some extent by the fact that both Gabriel and Mary have their hands crossed over their breasts, and it makes me think that the fresco shows, if not the moment of Christ's conception, then a split second before it. At other times it seems to me that perhaps the event is over and Gabriel is rising and on the point of leaving. John Ruskin (1819–1900) wrote of it:

> No gorgeous robe is upon her, no lifted throne set for her; the golden border gleams faintly on the dark blue dress; the seat is drawn into the shadow of a lowly loggia. The face is of no strange, far-sought loveliness; the features might even be thought hard, and they are worn with watching, and severe, though innocent. She stoops forward with her arms folded on her bosom: no casting down of eye nor shrinking of the frame in fear; she is too earnest, too self-forgetful for either: wonder and enquiry are there, but chastened and free from doubt; meekness, yet mingled with a patient majesty; peace, yet sorrowfully sealed, as if the promise of the angel were already underwritten by the prophecy of Simeon. They who pass and re-pass in the twilight of that solemn corridor need not the adjuration inscribed beneath: 'When you come before the face of the Virgin Inviolate, be sure to utter an *Ave* as you pass.'[7]

Agitation, reflection, enquiry and submission. But afterwards there was the joy of the Magnificat, and for a smiling Virgin who looks happy enough to sing it I turn to the Annunciation in the *Très riches heures du duc de Berry*, painted in about 1415 by the Limburg brothers.

Bible readings
Isaiah 7:10–14: A young woman shall conceive and bear a son.
1 John 1:1–2: That which was from the beginning.

Philippians 2:6–7: Taking the form of a servant, being born in the likeness of man.

Ephesians 1:9b–10: His purpose he set forth in Christ as a plan for the fullness of time.

John 1:14: And the word became flesh and dwelt among us.

Luke 1:26–38: Do not be afraid Mary, for you have found favour with God.

Intercessions

For those who suffer from skin disease and foot problems.

Thanksgiving for the work of religious artists, particularly that of Botticelli, Fra Filippo Lippi, Fra Angelico and the Limburg brothers.

Rejoicing in the Virgin Mary's cooperation in the divine plan of salvation.

Place of spiritual retreat

With Our Lady after the Annunciation, as in Luke 1.

APRIL

7 APRIL
St John Baptist de La Salle, priest (1651–1719)

CHERRY *Prunus avium* (sweet cherry); *prunus cerasus* (cooking cherry)

Cultivation notes

Both species are native to England, but the Romans introduced cultivated cherries from the Near East towards the end of the first century. Until recently it was not practical to grow a sweet cherry tree for fruit in the ordinary garden. First, it would reach about 40 feet in height; second, it would be self-sterile and so two trees would be needed. However, around 30 years ago the self-fertile 'Stella' was introduced, whilst the 'Colt' rootstock enabled trees to be controlled at 15–20 feet, and it became possible to maintain pyramids at 10 feet. Now there is the 'Compact Stella', which means that more of us can have the pleasure of home-produced cherries, either from a small manageable tree in the garden or from a dwarf subject in a pot on the patio. Other popular sweet cherries are 'Merton Bigarreau', 'Napoleon Bigarreau' and 'Van'. The growth of the cooking cherry is more compact, and the favourite 'morello' is self-fertile and begins to fruit at about three or four years of age. Both types of cherry can now be fan-trained against a wall. Netting to protect from birds will probably be necessary, wherever or however they are grown.

History and lore

Traditionally the cherry signifies 'good education', and this makes it appropriate for the founder of the Brothers of the Christian Schools. John Baptist was a notable pioneer in teacher-training, in the education of the

170

working classes and in the rehabilitation of delinquents. He was born in Reims and became a canon there at the age of 16. He studied at Saint-Sulpice from the age of 19 and was ordained priest in 1678. In collaboration with the layman Adam Nyel, he opened two schools for poor boys and then gave up his canonry and sold all his possessions to help with famine relief in the Champagne area. A further four schools were opened in spite of the difficulty in finding teachers. However, a group of 12 teachers eventually formed themselves into a religious community under his direction. Parish priests began to send young men to him to train as teachers, with the expectation that they would return to their villages to help with local education. As a result of this, in 1686 John Baptist established the first training college for teachers and two free schools in Paris, which met with great success. One of his most notable innovations was the replacement of one-to-one teaching in Latin with class teaching in the vernacular. He also instituted schools for disturbed boys and held Sunday schools that combined religious instruction with practical and technical training in crafts. He wrote two major works: *The Conduct of Christian Schools* laid out his methods and motivation, whilst *Meditations for Sundays* set forth his approach to prayer. He died at the age of 68 and was canonized in 1900. In 1950 he was made patron of schoolteachers.

Towards meditation
One of St John Baptist's rules was that children should remain silent during lessons, and whilst this goes against the grain of modern methodology one cannot help but admire a man, from the upper class himself, who provided schools for the poor in an age when their education in anything other that manual skills was widely considered to be unnecessary if not undesirable. Wherever possible the Church provides us with an opportunity to know the saints through their writings, and today, in the second Office reading, we find an extract from the *Meditations* of St John Baptist. It is addressed to teachers – and therefore to me – and brings me back to the root and purpose of my calling. He reminds me first of Paul's statement that the teacher is appointed by God in the Church and that ability to follow my calling comes from the Holy Spirit. As a teacher I am a minister of Jesus Christ, perform a holy service and should set my children an example of love, diligence and hard work. Following St Paul's urgings, I should be happy to be regarded as a servant and inspire my pupils by my own perseverance. As an ambassador of Christ I should write letters from him on their hearts. Finally, my patron reminds me that

as a teacher I am integral to the mission of the Church and that Christ himself helps me to bring to his kingdom those he has entrusted to my charge. I still believe this with all my heart and soul, in spite of the fact that in a secular school my work for him must be by example and never by precept.

Bible readings
Proverbs 1:8; 5:1; 23:26: Give me your heart and let your eyes observe my ways.
Ephesians 3:14–19: The love of Christ surpasses all knowledge.
Ephesians 4:1–13: His gifts were that some should become pastors and teachers.
2 Corinthians 3:1–6: You are a letter from Jesus Christ.
2 Timothy 4:1–5: Be unfailing in patience and in teaching.
Mark 10:13–16: Let the children come to me; do not hinder them.

Intercessions
For the Brothers of the Christian Schools and for all teachers.

Place of spiritual retreat
Listening to Christ's teaching, as in Mark 10.

21 APRIL
St Anselm, bishop and doctor (1033–1109)

CANTERBURY BELL *Campanula glomerata* 'Superba'

Cultivation notes
This perennial garden flower grows in any well-drained soil in sun or light shade. It is clump-forming and will achieve a height of 30 inches and a spread of three feet. The leaves grow in rosettes at the base and all the way up the stem. Rich purple-blue flowers appear in summer. Divide regularly in spring or autumn to propagate and to ensure the plants' health and strength.

History and lore
Anselm was born at Aosta in northern Italy and, after falling out with his profligate father, he moved first to Burgundy, where he lived with his

mother's family, and then, attracted by Lanfranc, to Normandy. There, aged about 27 and after a great deal of deliberation, he entered the Benedictine Abbey at Bec. He was made prior early in his monastic career and wrote his *De Grammatica* and *Prayers and Meditations*. These were followed, in 1077 and 1078, by the *Monologion* and *Proslogion*, the latter being famous for its 'ontological' argument for the existence of God. In 1078 Anselm was elected abbot and became closely associated with his former mentor Lanfranc, who had by then been archbishop of Canterbury for eight years. Lanfranc died in 1089 and Anselm succeeded him after four years, a delay caused by King William Rufus, who until then would not ratify the appointment. Anselm's time at Canterbury was marked by a series of disputes, first with William Rufus and then with Henry I. Like the later Thomas Becket he was intransigent on the Church's jurisdiction over spiritual matters, and this resulted in two periods of exile. During the first he wrote *Cur Deus Homo?* [Why God became Man]. From about 1106–7 until his death at almost 80, Anselm remained in England. Thomas Becket requested his canonization at Tours in 1163, and by about 1165 two feasts of Anselm were established at Canterbury. By the late twelfth century his cult had been overshadowed by Becket's own and it was not until 1720 that he was made a Doctor of the Church, and thus recognized as the most important Christian writer between Augustine of Hippo and Thomas Aquinas.

Towards meditation

I have chosen a campanula for Anselm because of his connections with Canterbury, reserving the wild species for Augustine, whom Anselm studied deeply during his early years as a monk at Bec. In his three major written works he justifies theological enquiry by following Augustine's method of faith seeking understanding. This is not the place to weigh the merits of Anselm's arguments, either for the existence of God or for a satisfactory reason as to why God became man. But I find great relevance in his motivation, and in his belief that reason can illuminate the coherence of Christian faith:

> I am not trying, Lord, to penetrate your sublimity, for my understanding is not up to that. But I long in some measure to understand your truth, which my heart believes and loves. For I am not seeking to understand in order to believe, but I believe in order that I may understand. For this too I believe: that unless I believe, I shall not understand.[8]

The humility of intention expressed here is present also in a further extract from the *Proslogion*, which forms today's second Office reading. Here Anselm's prayer is to know and love God, so that he may rejoice in him. But God is recognized as the 'supreme and inaccessible light', and Anselm acknowledges that his prayer cannot be answered fully in this life, so he asks for increasing knowledge day by day, that on earth his joy may be great in hope and reach its fullness in heaven.

I take it that Anselm's aim was to show that faith is reasonable, rather than to find reasons to prove that faith is justifiable. There is great joy for a Christian who sees an agreement between faith and reason. My confessor and I have often shared it, agreeing with each other that the faith *is* astonishing in its coherence, wonderfully woven and all of a piece, to the extent that we find it impossible not to believe. And so together we pray Anselm's prayer:

> Let my mind meditate on you, let my tongue speak of you, let my heart love you, let my mouth preach you. Let my soul hunger for you, let my flesh thirst for you, my whole being desire you, until I enter into the joy of the Lord, who is God, Three in One, blessed for ever. Amen.

Bible readings
Psalm 19: The precepts of the Lord are right, rejoicing the heart.
John 6:63: The words that I have spoken to you are spirit and life.
Psalm 37: The mouth of the righteous utters wisdom.
Psalm 119: O Lord, teach me thy statutes.
1 Corinthians 1:18–25: The word of the Cross is folly, but to us it is the power of God.
2 Timothy 1:13–14; 2:1–3: Keep as your pattern the sound teaching you have heard.
Mark 4:1–20: The Parable of the Sower, and Christ's explanation.

Intercessions
For unbelievers.
Thanksgiving for the writings of Anselm, and for our own faith.

Place of spiritual retreat
Listening to Christ teaching by the lakeside, as in Mark 4.

23 APRIL
St George, martyr, patron of England (d. c. 303)

ROSE 'SHAKESPEARE'
(David Austin)

Cultivation notes

This exceptional modern
English shrub rose has the
characteristics of a Gallica and
an excellent perfume. It is
repeat-flowering and the
blooms are deep red, turning
to purple with age. 'Shakespeare' reaches a height of about three feet.

History and lore

The story of George and the Dragon was popularized in the West through
the *Golden Legend*, translated and printed by Caxton. It is not frequently
mentioned nowadays that George allegedly promised to rid the 'king and
people' of the dragon on condition that they believe in Jesus and offer
themselves for baptism. The only reward he asked was that the king would
honour the Church and look after the poor. It is also rarely repeated that
the legend continues with an account of George's martyrdom at Lydda
during the persecution of Diocletian and Maximian, which is probably the
only factual element in the story. In England the cult of George goes back
at least to the seventh century, and he is mentioned in the Old English
martyrology and in those of Bede and the Irish Oengus. Aelfric also
repeated the legend. During the Crusades the cult took on huge
dimensions and Richard I put himself and his army under George's
protection, even though it was uncertain that the saint had been a soldier.
George became the personification of English Christian chivalry. Edward
III (1327–77) founded the Order of the Garter under his patronage, for
which St George's Chapel at Windsor was built by Edward IV and Henry
VII; and by the time Shakespeare wrote *Henry V* he could put into the
king's mouth the famous lines of encouragement: 'The game's afoot /
Follow your spirit; and, upon this charge / Cry "God for Harry! England
and Saint George!"' (Act III, scene i).

By the late Middle Ages, Venice, Genoa, Portugal and Catalonia
had adopted George as their patron, and the Irish Sea is still sometimes

THORN, FIRE AND LILY

called Saint George's Channel because a late version of the legend claims that he visited England, approaching it from the west. He was invoked against plague, leprosy and venereal disease, and remains patron of archers and armourers, and of farmers through a pun on *georgicus* (agricultural). The feast of George was reduced to a local one in 1969.

Towards meditation

Many English find it difficult to relate to George as their patron. His connection with medieval chivalry and outdated methods of warfare makes him an incongruous patron for a nation that now seems reluctant to vaunt its warlike and imperial past. Scotland has an apostle, and Wales and Ireland have saints connected with the beginnings of Christianity in their countries. There is considerable support in England for a change of patron, the main contenders being Alban, Protomartyr of England (20 June; third century); Edmund of East Anglia (20 November; 841–69); or Edward the Confessor (13 October; 1003–66). Nevertheless I choose an English red rose to commemorate George's martyrdom (and today, on his birth and death day, secretly elevate Shakespeare to a position of high honour – though perhaps not to sainthood).

In a reading from the sermons of Peter Damian (1006–72) the Divine Office dwells on the martyrdom of George, which complements our joy in the glory of Eastertide. George, says Peter, exchanged military service for the service of Christ, and gave away all he had to the poor. Whilst God handed over the body of his martyr to the murderers, he defended his soul with the unconquerable power of faith. But we must imitate the saint as well as admire him. We too must disregard possessions, for no one can put them first and 'fight properly and boldly for the faith'; we too must keep the goal of heaven in mind, whether or not 'the world smiles on us ... or menaces us with adversities'; we must lead godly lives and, in the clothing of our baptismal rebirth in Christ, put away our old life and, living the new, worthily celebrate the paschal mystery.

Bible readings

1 Peter 2:21–4: Christ suffered for you.
Romans 8:35–9: Who shall separate us from the love of Christ?
Psalm 11: In the Lord I take refuge.
Revelation 7:9–17: Behold a great multitude ... clothed in white robes.
2 Timothy 4:7–8: I have finished the race, I have kept the faith.

Philippians 3:8–10: I have suffered the loss of all things, and count them as refuse.

John 15:18–21: If the world hates you, know that it has hated me.

Intercessions

Thanksgiving for the work of rose-breeders.

For soldiers, archers, armourers, and farmers; for the people of England, Venice, Genoa, Portugal and Catalonia.

Thanksgiving for the martyrs, and for the writings of Peter Damian; for grace to follow his teaching.

Place of spiritual retreat

Listening to Christ's teaching, as in John 15.

25 APRIL
St Mark, evangelist (d. c. 74)

PRIMULA AURICULA 'MARK'

Cultivation notes

This alpine auricula is rosette-forming. The flat flowers have rounded petals and bloom in spring. They have pale cream centres and deep wine-purple-coloured petals fading to pink at the outer edges. The vivid green leaves are smooth and oval, and the plant reaches a height of 11 inches. It favours partial shade and moist soil, and is fully hardy.

History and lore

Mark, apparently a Jew and a native of Jerusalem, is normally identified as the young man clad only in a linen cloth who followed Christ from the Garden of Gethsemane and who, when seized, 'left the linen cloth and ran away naked' (Mark 14:51). Later, when Paul and Barnabas departed on the first mission to Cyprus, Mark accompanied them as far as Perga and then turned back towards Jerusalem. When Barnabas wanted Mark to go with them on the second journey, Paul refused to take someone he regarded as having deserted them the first time (Acts 15:38). The ensuing split between Paul and Barnabas led to the latter's preaching in Cyprus with Mark, while Paul took Silas as a companion (Acts 13 and 15). By the time of Colossians 4:10, when Paul was a prisoner, presumably in Rome,

Mark was with him. Paul must have forgiven him, because the text indicates that he intended to send Mark on a mission to Colossae. In Philemon 24 he is mentioned as being with the apostolic group that included Luke. From 2 Timothy 4:11 we learn that Mark is clearly with Timothy, and Paul values him sufficiently to say, 'Get Mark and bring him with you; for he is very useful in serving me.' In 1 Peter 5:13 the Apostle refers to Mark as 'my son', and this chimes with the tradition that Mark's Gospel represents Peter's teaching and recounts his memories. Clement of Alexandria (second century) supports the idea, but he does not mention – as later claimed by Eusebius (third century) – that Mark went to Alexandria. Nevertheless the tradition persists that Peter himself asked Mark to go to Alexandria to spread the word of God. Whilst he was celebrating an Easter Mass there, pagans slipped a noose around his neck, shouting, 'Let us drag this cowherd to the rubbish tip.' He was pulled through the streets of the town to prison, where Christ appeared to comfort him, saying, 'Peace be with you, Mark, my evangelist!' His relics were brought to Venice in the ninth century by two sea captains and he has been patron of the city ever since. The original church was destroyed in 976 and the present basilica rebuilt to house both the relics and a series of mosaics that date from the twelfth and thirteenth centuries and depict his life and death and the 'translation' (transfer) of his relics.

Towards meditation
The 'synoptic problem', that is, the debate about whether Matthew or Mark wrote the first gospel and who of the three evangelists, Matthew, Mark and Luke, copied from whom, is fascinating. One could spend the whole of Mark's feast reading up on it. But since I am not a biblical scholar and do not teach religion, and furthermore since the debate is still not resolved, there would be little spiritual or practical point. It may instead prove valuable to consider how the *nature* of Mark's Gospel makes it different from the others.

From the moment we first meet him, ostensibly in Chapter 14 of his own Gospel, Mark seems to me a man of action and of abrupt decisions. We are not told why he turned back to Jerusalem on the first journey, but, if it was weakness, he certainly made up for it later. Whereas Matthew's Gospel is formal and concentrates on Jesus as the long-awaited Messiah, Mark's is full of life and action. He is concerned with what Jesus did and with the places he went to, rather than with what he taught. He does stress, however, Christ's teaching that the Son of Man must suffer and that the disciples must be prepared to follow him. Jesus is to be understood as the crucified Saviour, and Mark would have been well aware of his own people's difficulty in accepting a Messiah who chose humility and suffering and who would not be seen as the King of Glory until his second coming. If Mark did indeed hear the story direct from Peter, this would certainly explain the vividness of his Gospel. It is of course the shortest and the roughest in style, but in spite of this it contains in its 16 chapters a surprising amount of colourful and circumstantial detail. And where the synoptic Gospels do overlap, Mark's accounts tend to be the longest. It is clear too that Mark, as an active apostle, had Gentile readers in mind, often explaining Jewish customs. It has been suggested that the brevity of Mark is explained by haste and the need to pare away all but the essentials in the teaching of new converts. The good news begins with the voice of John the Baptist, in fulfilment of Isaiah, crying out from the desert that the nation should prepare for God's coming. The four evangelists show us Christ in their own characteristic way. He could not have been captured in a single portrait. Today I thank God for the one Mark has given us. As an active man himself, so he presents his Lord. And if his Gospel was indeed the first, without it we might not have had Matthew or Luke either.

Bible readings
Psalm 89: I will sing of thy steadfast love, O Lord, for ever.
1 Corinthians 1:23–4: We preach Christ crucified who is the power and the wisdom of God.
2 Timothy 1:8–9: Share in suffering for the gospel.
Colossians 1:3–6: The word of truth, the gospel that has come to you.
Acts 5:12–32: Imprisonment of Apostles in the Early Church.
1 Peter 5:5–14: My son Mark sends you greetings.
Matthew 28:20: I am with you always, to the close of the age.
Mark 16:15–20: Go into all the world and preach the gospel.

Intercessions
Thanksgiving for the Gospel and apostleship of Mark.

Place of spiritual retreat
With the disciples after the Ascension of Christ, as at the end of Mark's Gospel.

NOTES

PART 1

1. Jane Mossendew, *Gardening with God: Light in Darkness* (London: Continuum/Burns & Oates, 2002).
2. C.A. Johns, *Flowers of the Field* (London: Routledge, 1913).
3. Nicholas Culpeper, *Complete Herbal* (London: Foulsham, n.d.).
4. See W.E. Addis and T. Arnold, *A Catholic Dictionary* (London: Virtue, 1928).
5. *The Language of Flowers*: a compilation of various Victorian writers. See Lesley Gordon, *Green Magic* (London: Webb & Bower, 1977).
6. Sutton and Sons, *The Culture of Vegetables and Flowers* (London: Simpkin, 1904).
7. See Introduction to Jane Mossendew, *Gardening with God*.
8. Divine Office, Friday, Week Three, Morning Prayer.
9. From Edwin Arlington Robinson (1869–1935), 'Veteran Sirens', in Louis Untermeyer (ed.), *The Albatross Book of Living Verse* (London: Collins, n.d.).
10. Katherine Oldmeadow, *The Folklore of Herbs* (Birmingham: Cornish Bros, 1946).
11. Tate and Brady, new version 1696.
12. Samuel Pepys, *Diary* (London: Latham & Matthews, 1970–83).
13. Margaret Baker, *Folklore and Customs of Rural England* (Newton Abbot: David & Charles, 1974).
14. In Felicitas Corrigan OSB, *A Benedictine Tapestry* (London: Darton, Longman & Todd, 1991).
15. Richard Mabey, *Flora Britannica* (London: Chatto & Windus, 1998).
16. Mrs M. Grieve, *A Modern Herbal* (Harmondsworth: Penguin, 1976).
17. Deni Bown, *Encyclopaedia of Herbs and Their Uses* (London: Dorling Kindersley, 1995).
18. Robert Frost, 'Mending Wall', in Ian Hamilton (ed.), *Robert Frost: Selected Poems* (London: Penguin, 1975).
19. Revd Hugh Macmillan, *Bible Teaching in Nature* (London: Macmillan, 1878).
20. Revd Jonathan Swift, *A Tale of a Tub* (London, 1704).

21. Julian of Norwich, *Revelations of Divine Love*, ed. Clifton Wolters OSB (Harmondsworth: Penguin, 1966).

22. G.K. Chesterton, 'The Donkey', in Robert Lynd (ed.), *An Anthology of Modern Verse* (London: Methuen, 1933).

23. G.S. Tyack, *Lore and Legend of the English Church* (London: William Andrews, 1899).

24. F. Nigel Hepper, *Illustrated Encyclopaedia of Bible Plants* (London: Intervarsity Press, 1992).

25. William Langland, from 'The Harrowing of Hell', 'The Vision of Piers Plowman', trans. Ronald Tamplin, in Ruth Etchells (ed.), *Early English Poets* (Oxford: Lion Publishing, 1988).

26. Joseph Mary Plunkett, 'I see his Blod Upon the Rose', in Patrick Murray (ed.), *The Deer's Cry* (Blackrock: Four Courts Press, 1986).

27. Anon., 'Woefully Arrayed' (British Museum Hailey MS, c. 1450), in *The Faber Book of Religious Verse* (London: Faber & Faber, 1972).

28. *Favourite Gregorian Chant*, EMI Classics for Pleasure; polyphonic settings on a Naxos disc by the Oxford Camerata, conducted by Jeremy Summerly.

29. William Langland, from 'The Vision of Piers Plowman', trans. Ronald Tamplin, in Etchells (ed.), *Early English Poets*.

PART 2

1. Maggie Campbell-Culver, *The Origin of Plants* (London: Hodder & Stoughton, 2001).

2. See Hilary of Poitiers, in Jane Mossendew, *Gardening with God*, p. 217.

3. HDRA, Ryton Organic Gardens, Coventry CV8 3LG.

4. Adapted by Mrs C.F. Alexander (1818–95) in *The New English Hymnal* (Norwich: Canterbury Press).

5. Mark Elvins, *Catholic Trivia* (London: HarperCollins, 1992).

6. St Augustine, *De Trinitate*, Vol. 4, Chapter 5.

7. In Maisie Ward, *The Splendour of the Rosary* (London: Sheed & Ward, 1946).

8. St Anselm, *Proslogion*, 1.

INDEX

INDEX

Pink, Maiden   78
Potato   154
Primula auricula 'Mark'   177

Reed, common   45
Rose 'Shakespeare'   175
Rue   99

Sage   58
Shamrock   157
Soapwort   62
Speedwell   90
Spikenard   122
Sweet corn   96

Trefoil, lesser   157
Tulip 'Fidelio'   153

Veronica, Hebe   90
   Speedwell   90
Vine   50, 87
Violet, Sweet   75
   Water   93

Wheat   96
Willow, Crack   82
   'Pussy'   77
Wormwood   39

184